Painter 11 Creativity

To my mum, Margaret, who inspired me to be an artist and follow my passion for art, and to Frankie Manning, who inspired me to dance the Lindy Hop and to take joy in every moment.

Painter 11 Creativity: Digital Artist's Handbook

Jeremy Sutton

AMSTERDAM • BOSTON • HEIDELBERG • LONDON • NEW YORK • OXFORD • PARIS
SAN DIEGO • SAN FRANCISCO • SINGAPORE • SYDNEY • TOKYO

Focal Press is an imprint of Elsevier

Focal Press is an imprint of Elsevier
Linacre House, Jordan Hill, Oxford OX2 8DP, UK
30 Corporate Drive, Suite 400, Burlington, MA 01803, USA

First edition 2010

Notices

Knowledge and best practice in this field are constantly changing. As new research and experience broaden our understanding, changes in research methods, professional practices, or medical treatment may become necessary.

Practitioners and researchers must always rely on their own experience and knowledge in evaluating and using any information, methods, compounds, or experiments described herein. In using such information or methods they should be mindful of their own safety and the safety of others, including parties for whom they have a professional responsibility.

To the fullest extent of the law, neither the Publisher nor the authors, contributors, or editors, assume any liability for any injury and/or damage to persons or property as a matter of products liability, negligence or otherwise, or from any use or operation of any methods, products, instructions, or ideas contained in the material herein.

British Library Cataloguing in Publication Data
Sutton, Jeremy
   painter 11 creativity: digital artist's handbook
   1. Corel painter
   004.6'89-dc22

Library of Congress Control Number: 2009934161

ISBN: 978-0-240-81255-7

For information on all Focal Press publications
visit our website at focalpress.com

Printed and bound in Canada
09 10 11 12 11 10 9 8 7 6 5 4 3 2 1

Contents

5   Painting From Photos II—Brushwork   107

6   Painting From Photos III—Completion   143

7   Going for it with Color!   167

Collage Portraiture—The Art of Combining Multiple Images into a Portrait 189

 Gallery   221

Appendix

Foreword

In the words of Spinal Tap's legendary Nigel Tufnel, "It goes to *eleven*." Corel Painter 11, that is. And with this release, Jeremy has written the 4th edition of *Painter Creativity*. Painter continues to be recognized as the gold standard for expressive natural-media software, just as Jeremy represents the gold standard for teaching aspiring artists to express themselves through this digital tool.

The world of Painter (now 18 years young) has matured over the past few years. It now has its own magazine. In the world of portrait photography, it has become a standard tool. Combined with ink-jet printing and canvas, artists are embellishing Painter art with traditional media. There are many web sites—including Jeremy's PaintboxJ.com—dedicated to Painter as a primary expressive tool. On social networking sites like *Twitter* and *MySpace*, Painter is a regular topic of discussion.

Painter has evolved to include a deep tool set with a wide range of expressive media types. Jeremy has kept pace with its advances and utilizes these tools to give direction to his students' personal odysseys. As through dance, Jeremy utilizes Painter as an expressive medium through which he reveals his zest for life. He is an excellent guide to aid you in finding your unique creative voice in the form of style.

Jeremy was among the initial wave of Painter aficionados. I remember seeing him at the 1993 Digital Be-In one evening during Macworld in San Francisco, entertaining the crowds with his soon-to-be famous portraiture sessions. He was using Painter! I was intrigued and watched for several minutes until I got an opportunity to speak with him. His enthusiasm was immediately apparent. He was full of questions about various aspects of Painter's inner workings. It was obvious that he possessed an innate understanding of Painter's expressive tools.

Over the years, Jeremy has been one of Painter's principal goodwill ambassadors. His good-natured enthusiasm has been responsible for launching many on their creative odysseys, with Painter acting as their compass. Jeremy has taken both his enthusiasm and teaching experience and poured it into these pages. And you, now holding this book, are about to be the beneficiary of his efforts. If you are considering starting, or are already on your own creative odyssey, you couldn't be in better hands.

Congratulations go to Jeremy for this, the 4th edition of *Painter Creativity*, and to you—the reader and seeker of creative expression via Painter. Indeed, may your personal odyssey take you to *eleven*.

John Derry
May 2009
Omaha, Nebraska

Portrait of John Derry created by Jeremy Sutton (using Fractal Design Painter 2) at the 1992 SIGGRAPH trade show in Chicago.

Acknowledgements and Contributors

I thank the wonderful team at Focal Press who helped make this book a reality, especially my editors Valerie Geary and David Albon.

Thank you to the great teams of people at Corel and Wacom who have produced such amazing art tools for artists like me, and who have been so supportive and encouraging over the years. Many of you have become good friends and are always such a pleasure to work with. Thanks to Mark Zimmer and the late Tom Hedges for creating Painter, to John Derry for helping shape it into what it is today, to Robert MacDonald, Kelly Manuel, David Toeg and my other friends at Corel, and to Mr Yamada, Jim McCartney, Doug Little, Michael Marcum, Peter Dietrich, Tom Lam, Helen Deng, Izumi Tosa and my other friends at Wacom.

Thank you to Peggy (www.PeggyGyulai.com) for being such a loving and supportive sounding board for bouncing ideas off, for sharing so much of her own talent, expertise and experience, and for taking the time to read over my manuscript, as well as keeping me well caffeinated!

Thank you to my mum, Margaret, and sister Debbi, both artists whose wise words, advice and critiques over the years have undoubtedly contributed to the artistic approach I share in this book. Thanks to the rest of my family who are always encouraging, supportive and happy to offer opinions whenever asked, and who are by now used to me writing my books while on travels in the UK!

Thank you to the many thousands of students whom I have had the pleasure of teaching over the last 15 years for your inspiration and enthusiasm. Wishing you all the best with your continued creative development.

Thank you to those who have been the subjects of, and inspiration for, the paintings featured in this book, and to those who have generously shared their thoughts and advice.

Thank you to all the contributors who have so generously shared their creativity in this book, including all those (listed below) who kindly permitted me to include their custom brushes within the JeremyFaves2 brush category contained in the attached resource CD and who contributed to the Student Gallery.

David Christensen
www.northlightproducts.com
Advice and assistance on color management

Henk Dawson
www.henkdawson.com
Student Gallery contributing artist

Scott Dupras
www.scottdupras.com
Custom brushes

Lois Freeman-Fox
http://web.me.com/lois.stuart/Lois_Freeman-Fox_Artist_Film_Editor
Student Gallery contributing artist

Sam Gray
www.samgrayportraits.com
Student Gallery contributing artist

Peggy Gyulai
www.peggygyulai.com
Input, advice and assistance on the use of acrylics and oils and on traditional color palette
creation. Custom color set

Denise Laurent
www.imagine.co.uk
Custom brushes

Jolyn Montgomery
www.jolynmontgomery.com
Student Gallery contributing artist

Paulo Roberto Purim
www.jogodeluz.com.br
Custom brushes

Larry Salveson
www.softwarepursuits.com
Advice on Windows PC issues, including the tips about showing hidden files and folders

Sherron Sheppard
www.sheppardphotography.com
Custom brushes and color sets

Laurie Solomon
Advice on resolution issues

About the Author

Corel Painter Master Jeremy Sutton is a world-renowned artist, author and educator. Originally from London, UK, he now resides in San Francisco, California. The author of six books, five instructional video/DVD sets and the founder of the educational web site PaintboxJ.com, Jeremy is a respected expert on Painter, speaking at numerous conferences, teaching workshops in his Sutton Studios & Gallery and across the globe, and being part of the worldwide group of artists invited to join the Corel Painter alpha test team.

Jeremy brings a unique combination of artistic and technical experience to his teachings. He has drawn for over 40 years and studied drawing, sculpture and printmaking at the Ruskin School of Drawing and Fine Art in Oxford, UK, and drawing and lithography at the Vrijie Akademie in The Hague, the Netherlands. His colorful portraits have been published and exhibited internationally, and are in numerous private and public collections. Balancing his grounding in the traditional arts is Jeremy's experience as a scientist, which includes earning a Masters degree in Physics from Oxford University and working for 12 years in the field of superconducting magnets and low temperature research systems. Jeremy has been a full-time professional artist since 1994.

To learn more about Jeremy and his art, workshops, publications and resources, visit www.JeremySutton.com and www.PaintboxJ.com.

Introduction

Goals

Welcome to the wonderful world of digital painting! This book is designed to empower you creatively and to help you stretch your artistic muscles. The goals of the instruction I share within these pages are two-fold:

1 to provide you with a sound and thorough technical foundation and deep understanding of the powerful tools of digital painting, such that the computer becomes invisible as you paint; and

2 to share with you an expressive, open and improvisational approach to making art that balances structure with spontaneity.

The mastery of media and tools involves getting to know, becoming familiar with, and understanding the behaviors, mechanics and capabilities of those tools, whether in the computer or not. I want you to push the tools to the edge, find where the limitations are, and be in control of them. The technical information and structure you will learn frees you up to be spontaneous and improvisational. Think beyond one media, effect, formula, recipe or technique and think instead of entering a journey of improvised transformation that will mix, blend and combine all sorts of techniques and media, and will be different for every painting. Every image suggests its own unique path of transformation. Continually experiment. Allow yourself to be free, intuitive and spontaneous, to "feel the groove." Embrace serendipity and treat every unexpected result as an opportunity to explore a direction you may not have previously considered. Be open-minded and allow your creativity to flow.

Digital Painting in Context

Before we dive into the nitty gritty of tools, techniques and process, let's take a step back and look at digital painting in the context of art in general. What is digital painting? My friend and client Bob Pritikin is fond of saying: "all art made by the use of the digits on our hands, from finger painting onwards, is digital art."

Digital art is commonly associated with art made up of distinct picture elements, or "pixels." In that case you could consider Chuck Close's dramatic portraits, built up from arrays of small square or triangular drawings, as "digital" since they are made up of hand-drawn pixels. The pointillists such a George Seurat can also be considered to have painted with pixels. In both these cases the human visual perception system of an observer at a distance performs a blending, mixing and interpretation in the brain that results in seeing a relatively smooth image and knowing exactly what is being represented in the paintings. If that same observer views the artworks from close up, they appear abstract.

In today's context *digital painting* is usually associated with the process of painting on a computer, often using tools such as a pressure-sensitive Wacom tablet and pen, and Corel Painter software. In this case the image is electronic data—ones and zeros on a computer chip or disc. A digital painting is initially visually manifested on a computer display as an array of colored pixels. Just as with pointillist paintings, the human visual perception system efficiently blends and interprets the pixels so that typically we see smooth gradations of tone and color. A digital painting can be physically manifested on a solid substrate, like paper or canvas, through use of a printer.

From time to time you may hear the term "computer-generated" art. The digital painting referred to in this book is no more "computer generated" than a Van Gogh painting was "oil brush generated." It involves original handmade brush strokes on a digital canvas. The act of digital painting is very similar to the act of traditional painting, only with electronic media instead of physical media (and much less mess to clear up).

Let's compare digital paint to physical paint. Within Corel Painter you have literally hundreds of brushes that emulate a multitude of natural/physical/traditional (choose your term) mark-making media, including Oil, Pastel, Pencil, Watercolor, Gouache, Acrylic, and much more. Thus Painter, and by extension digital paint, is not a single art medium, it is many art media. Digital paint is a collection of art media that are applied and manipulated on the computer. It was only 40 years ago that acrylic paint was the revolutionary "new" medium that some looked down upon as not "real," or "too easy"—the same criticism now occasionally heard being leveled against digital painting. Digital painting in the electronic realm has evolved since computer pioneer Douglas C. Engelbart's seminal demonstration of the first graphical user interface in San Francisco in 1968. Digital painting is now established as a respected and accepted medium, or collection of media, with digital paintings being exhibited in galleries and museums worldwide.

I view digital painting as a part of my art creation process, a process that begins the moment I see a subject and visualize a painting. The process continues through the way I compose and capture a moment in the camera lens, if I am using photography, and may involve both digital and physical paint, before a completed artwork emerges. I describe my completed artwork as a painting, not a digital painting or computer art. The literal description, as I may put on a label in an exhibition, depends on the media I use. An example is: "pigment ink and acrylic on canvas."

The bottom line is that digital paint is just another art medium (or collection of media), albeit an immensely powerful, efficient, versatile, non-allergenic, non-toxic and fun medium to use.

Your Digital Painting Toolbox

Corel Painter is your digital art studio in your computer. It is a complement to, not a competitor with, Adobe Photoshop, your digital darkroom. I recommend, as a minimum, that your digital painting toolbox includes both Painter and Photoshop.

A Wacom graphics tablet, with pressure-sensitive pen, is the key interface between artist and computer that allows you to make art on the computer. The root of "Wacom" is "Wa," a Japanese word for harmony, and "com" for computer—the harmony between human and computer. Unlike a mouse, which is relativistic, a tablet is absolute. Every point on the tablet active area corresponds to a unique point on the screen.

Wacom offers three main categories of tablets to choose from:

1 The Bamboo tablets—these are designed for consumer and office use. They are inexpensive and anyone using a computer should at least have such a tablet, even if they do no art or graphics. However, for the artist I recommend you invest in one of the professional models, either an Intuos4 or Cintiq.

2 The Inutos4 series tablets—they come in small, medium, large and, you guessed, extra large. I'd recommend the medium for use with a laptop, especially if you will be traveling with your tablet a lot. The medium and up are all excellent for use with a studio or home based computer. The extra large is perfect for use with an Apple 30 inch Cinema HD display.

3 The Cintiq series tablets—the Cintiqs combine a display and tablet in one. The Cintiqs are very intuitive. The smaller model, the Cintiq 12WX, is excellent for presentations, teaching, live artwork and performance. The larger Cintiq 21UX is a good studio tablet, large enough to see your art in detail.

To find out more information and about pricing, you can visit the respective manufacturer web sites, www.corel.com and www.wacom.com. In my online education store at www.paintboxj.com you will also find links with special pricing.

What's New and Improved in Corel Painter 11?

If you already have an older version of Painter and you are wondering if it is worth upgrading to Painter 11, the simple answer is: yes, absolutely! Just the increased speed of Painter 11, almost six times as fast as Painter X for some brushes, makes it worthwhile. In addition the new Hard Media brushes, like the new Real 6B Soft Pencil, are fabulous and are well worth the upgrade. Besides these two key reasons, there are also expandable Color and Mixer palettes, improved color management that allows you to work in Adobe RGB (1998) and maximize the color consistency between Painter and Photoshop, file support for PNG files, improved selection tools, more powerful layer palette interactions and, last but not least, a built-in menu command to email your paintings. For more specifics visit www.corel.com/painter. Regarding the backward compatibility of instructions in this book, since the interface has not changed significantly between Painter X and Painter 11 most of the instructions can be applied to earlier versions of Painter. However, I still recommend getting Painter 11, which will allow you to enjoy the full extent of what I share in the book.

What's New and Improved in the Wacom Intuos4?

The key improvements in the Wacom Intuos4 tablets over earlier models are:

1 Increased resolution (double that of the Intuos3).
2 Increased pressure sensitivity at the lowest pressure range (which makes a big difference in painting).
3 LED displays that show you what shortcut each ExpressKey is programmed for. This is particularly useful when you program special settings for different applications.
4 Finger-sensitive Touch Ring control that can be set to have up to four functions.
5 Radial menus that allow you to program an unlimited number of keyboard shortcuts that you can access without touching the keyboard,
6 Ergonomic design with a convenient ambidextrous tablet which keeps the ExpressKeys and Touch Ring to one side, and a comfortable grip pen with handy holder that stores all your extra nibs.
7 Slightly resistant surface that emulates the "tooth" of a natural surface, giving a more realistic and comfortable painting experience.

Together these changes add up to a powerful tool for painting that I highly recommend. Try one out and feel the difference for yourself.

What's New and Improved in this *Painter 11 Creativity* Book?

Painter 11 Creativity: Digital Artist's Handbook is the fourth edition of this series, which started in 2003 with the *Painter 8 Creativity: Digital Artist's Handbook*. The origin of the series was the curriculum I developed for my online class called *Beyond the Brush*. I am continuously refining and changing my workflow in Painter and this is reflected in all my teachings, including this book. In this edition I address questions, such as how I do post-print painting, that I am asked in my workshops and via email. This edition also includes a detailed explanation of how I set up the new Wacom Intuos4 tablet. I have endeavored to keep my instructions concise, relevant, to the point and easy to follow. My goal is to include only information that will move you forward in mastering Painter and empower your creativity. As with my original edition six years ago, this book is intended to be both a valuable self-study tool as well as a textbook for my workshops and for digital painting classes everywhere. Be reassured if you already own an earlier edition—you'll get enough new information from this latest edition to make it a worthwhile investment.

Cross Platform Compatibility

All instruction within this book is designed to be suitable for both Macintosh (Mac) and Windows Vista/XP (PC) operating systems. When a keyboard shortcut is mentioned, the Mac shortcut is followed by the PC shortcut, separated by a forward slash. For example, the shortcut for Save As in Painter (same as in Photoshop) is Cmd-Shift-S (Mac)/Ctrl-Shift-S (PC). I use "Cmd" to signify the Command, or Apple, key on the Macintosh keyboard. If a keyboard shortcut is mentioned without reference to either Mac or PC then assume it is the same in both platforms. Most screen shots show a Mac interface, since that is the main platform I use. Visually and functionally Painter is almost identical on either Mac or PC. There are a few menu commands that are in different places, such as Corel Painter 11 > Preferences (Mac)/Edit > Preferences (PC). I include a separate PC screen shot where warranted.

Occasionally I am asked about Mac versus PC. I recommend a Mac for creating art due to the Mac's "plug and play" ease of use and intuitive interface, and the excellent support, training and customer service offered through the Apple Stores.

For consistency I adopt the American spelling conventions throughout this book, so expect to see "color," not "colour." The exception is the Art of Making Marks Interview featured on the CD where Ric Holland's original Australian spellings have been preserved. Wherever possible I adopt the terminology used within Painter to describe palettes, menu items, commands, and so on.

Subject Matter

As you may have noticed if you have already flipped through the book, or are already familiar with my work, my work is primarily portraiture. I realize that there are many potential readers of this book who paint completely different subject matter, ranging from abstracts and fantasy scenes to animal portraiture, landscapes and cityscapes, some of which are reflected in the Appendix: Student Gallery. No matter what subject matter you like to depict and what style you work in, you will still find a lot of valuable information and techniques within this book. The fundamentals and workflow can be applied to any subject or style.

How to Get the Most Out of This Book

This book assumes that you know how to install and update your Wacom drivers and Corel Painter software, find the Control Panels, locate your application folders, find and select files on your hard drive and external discs, select and copy files, save, create and name files and folders, click and drag, double click, perform keyboard shortcuts where you hold down one or more keys while clicking others, and open, hide and close applications. If you are not confident in any of these basic computer skills I recommend you take a basic computer class before attempting to follow the instructions in this book.

This book does not make any assumptions about prior experience of using a Wacom tablet or Corel Painter or about having any art training.

Here are some tips for getting the most out of this book:

1 Don't Undo! Be committed to your marks and allow every mark you make on the canvas to add to the organic richness of your artwork. By not Undoing you will free the forward flow of your painting process.

2 Be bold. Take risks on the digital (and non-digital) canvas. Treat the exercises in this book as an opportunity to experiment. Don't worry about what others think. Don't expect to produce masterpieces right away. Plan to make many starts and studies.

3 Use your Wacom tablet and pen, not your mouse, trackball or trackpad. Put your mouse away for painting. Get in the habit of using your tablet for every activity you need to do on the computer. It is healthier (reduces repetitive stress injuries). The more you use a tablet the more like an extension of yourself it becomes.

4 Skim the whole book first to get a sense of the overview and where we are headed. Then go back and start following the detailed instructions and exercises in the order they appear.

If you are really keen to move ahead quickly and hone your skills, then the following power tips are also useful:

  i Use the book in conjunction with my DVDs and with my tutorial videos on www.paintboxj.com. Also explore the Painter resource links you'll find on www.paintercreativity.com. These links lead to the web sites of various Painter forums, teachers and artists.

 ii Attend my workshops (see www.jeremysutton.com for schedule).

iii Make a habit to regularly visit galleries and museums and carefully observe paintings in real life—see what works and why. Note how different artists compose their paintings using paint, color, tone and contrast.

iv If you are not a trained artist, take a traditional (that is, non-digital) drawing class. Carry a sketchbook with you at all times and get in the sketching habit. After a year of drawing take a traditional painting class. Any traditional art training you do will inform what you do in Painter, even when working from photographic reference.

Wishing you much enjoyment!

Jeremy Sutton

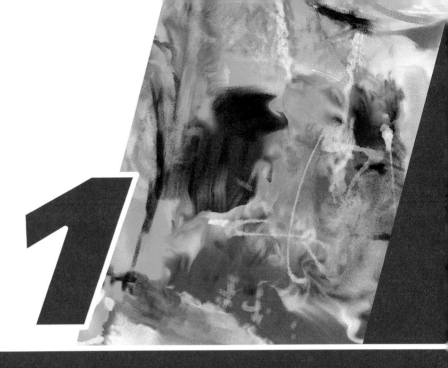

1

Get Ready

Fasten Your Seat Belt!

You are about to join, or continue on, a great journey of creative exploration, experimentation and expression. I hope this Handbook serves a useful and inspirational guide that will help you get over some of the bumps in the road and accelerate your creative growth into uncharted territories.

Before the fun bit of this journey, when you actually get to mess around with paint and spill pixels on your clothes, you first need to get ready for action. Put your seat belt on for the dull, techy, preparative stuff. That's what this first chapter is about. I assure you that the pain is worth it for the dramatic gain. Once you have organized your computer, programmed your Wacom tablet, installed the extra brushes and art materials, and optimized your Painter workspace, everything else flows much smoother.

If you are an advanced Painter user and have already programmed your tablet and installed extra brushes and art materials, and followed my set up from my other books, DVDs or PaintboxJ, then I suggest you briefly skim this chapter for anything new and move on to the next chapter. For those who are new to Painter, I recommend you try out my suggestions and adopt what works best for you.

System Requirements

Let's start with the minimum system requirements recommended by Corel for running Corel Painter 11. These are:

Mac Specific

Mac OS × 10.4 or 10.5 (with latest revision)
Power Mac® G5, 700 MHz or greater

PC Specific

Windows Vista® or Windows® XP (with latest Service Pack)
Pentium® IV, 700 MHz or greater

Mac or PC

1 GB of RAM
500 MB of hard disk space for installation
24-bit color display
1024 × 768 screen resolution

Please note these are the minimum requirements and you will be better off with more RAM and a faster computer which will give you better performance and help your creative process flow more smoothly. The approach to digital painting that I share in this book involves saving many uniquely named versions of your working file as you develop your artwork. A typical project of mine, such as the example of *Skycap Keith*, the painting reproduced on the cover of this book, can end up with 50–70 saved working image versions, and the project folder can end up containing anywhere from 2 to 15 GB of data. Thus I recommend that you aim to have, as a minimum, at least 25–50 GB of free storage space available. I recommend, in general, regularly updating your operating system and software (on the Mac go to apple menu > Software Update).

While the minimum recommended screen resolution is 1024 × 768 pixels, I recommend using as large a screen as you can accommodate and afford, such as the 30 inch flat panel Apple Cinema HD Display (2560 × 1600 pixel resolution), which works with Macs, Windows PC and graphics cards that support DVI ports.

Computer System Fine-Tuning

By optimizing the way your computer, tablet and painting software work together as a team, you creatively empower yourself on the digital canvas.

Mac Specific

For convenience I recommend adding two shortcuts into your Mac Finder browser sidebar. The first shortcut is for the Corel Painter 11 application folder. Locate this folder in your Applications folder and then drag it into the Places section of your Finder sidebar. You'll see an icon titled "Corel Painter 11." This shortcut is very useful anytime you are trying to locate extra art materials (color sets, papers, patterns and nozzles) copied into the Corel Painter 11 application folder > Support Files folder, as well as when you are copying extra brushes into your Painter Brushes folder.

The second shortcut I recommend is for hard drive > user folder > Library > Application Support > Corel > Painter 11. Drag this Painter 11 folder into the Places section of your Finder sidebar. You'll see an icon titled "Painter 11." This second shortcut will be useful whenever you wish to back up or copy the actual files for custom brush variants you create, which are located within the hard drive > user folder > Library > Application Support > Corel > Painter 11 > relevant workspace > Brushes > Painter Brushes > Brush Category folder.

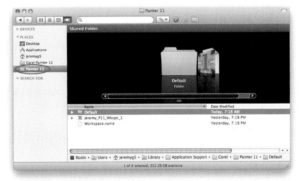

Figure 1.1 Shortcuts in the Finder browser sidebar (Mac).

When in the Finder, select Finder > Preferences and click on the Advanced tab. Make sure the "Show all file extensions" checkbox is checked. The file extension is valuable information when looking through Painter project files. There is a useful "Calculate all sizes" setting that allows you to see the total size (in MB or GB) of your project folders when you view them in the Finder browser. To choose this setting select View > Show View Options (Cmd-J); check "Calculate all sizes" and click on "Use as Defaults."

PC Specific

In Windows Vista, go to the Start > Control Panel and select Folder Options. In Windows XP, go to the Start > Settings > Control Panel and select Folder Options. You can also get to this dialog from Windows Explorer or My Computer using the menu Tools > Folder Options. Click on the View tab. Activate the radio button "Show hidden files and folders" and remove the check from "Hide extension for known file types," both in the advanced settings area. By showing hidden folders you will be able to see the custom data in your user directory and back up your custom brush variants. Seeing the extensions for files is useful in Painter since, for certain projects, you will want to know whether you are opening a RIFF or TIFF file.

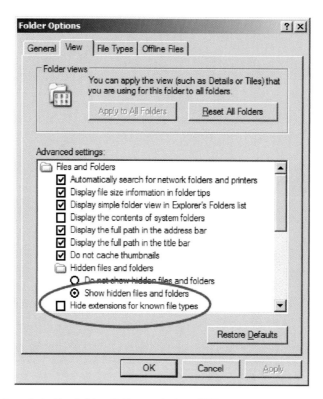

Figure 1.2 Adjustments in the Folder Options window (PC).

Wacom Tablet Customization

The instructions given here are based on the Wacom Intuos4 model. If you have an Intuos3 or Cintiq tablet the majority of the ExpressKey programming instructions can still be applied to those models as well. The Bamboo tablets do not have the same degree of customizability that the Intuos and Cintiq models offer.

Wacom Driver

Once you have connected your Wacom tablet to your computer, visit www.wacom.com, select your location and language, click on the Support tab and under Driver Download select your

Model Number and Operating System. Update your Wacom driver. It is worthwhile checking back regularly to see if there is an update to the driver for your model. On the same Support page you'll also find useful tutorial videos on customizing and using the various tablet models.

Stroke Nib

Remove the standard Wacom Intuos4 Grip Pen nib—a small, solid, white plastic rod—from your Wacom Grip Pen (you can use the nib removal device provided by Corel or your teeth). Replace it with the stroke nib, found in the pen holder (which unscrews to reveal a convenient container for the extra nibs). The stroke nib has a tiny spring in it. Insert the spring end into the pen. The stroke nib adds a little "softness" to the feel of the pen on the tablet. You can always replace it with the default nib at any time if you wish.

Additional Pens

If you have multiple users making use of your tablet you may wish to purchase additional Grip Pens so that each user has their own individual pen. The Intuos4 Grip Pens can be conveniently color-coded by installing different colored rings (stored in the pen holder) into the tip area. The advantage of different users having their own pens is that the tablet will recognize each pen and automatically apply that user's custom settings. Two other alternative pens that may be worth purchasing are the Intuos4 Art Pen, which provides rotational sensitivity, and the Intuos4 Airbrush, which includes an airbrush style finger wheel.

Physical Comfort

Being physically comfortable is an important aspect of freeing yourself up to be creative. Here are some basic suggestions to help you set up a comfortable and healthy physical workspace and develop healthy working habits. These suggestions are not intended to replace the advice of a health professional.

1 Adjust your chair height such that your feet are comfortably planted on the ground or on a suitable resting surface.
2 Face your computer screen head-on at 90 degrees, not at an oblique angle that forces you to twist your body or neck.
3 Avoid having a bright light source, such as a window, directly behind your screen.
4 Adjust your screen height such that your eyes are at the same level, or slightly above, the center of your screen.

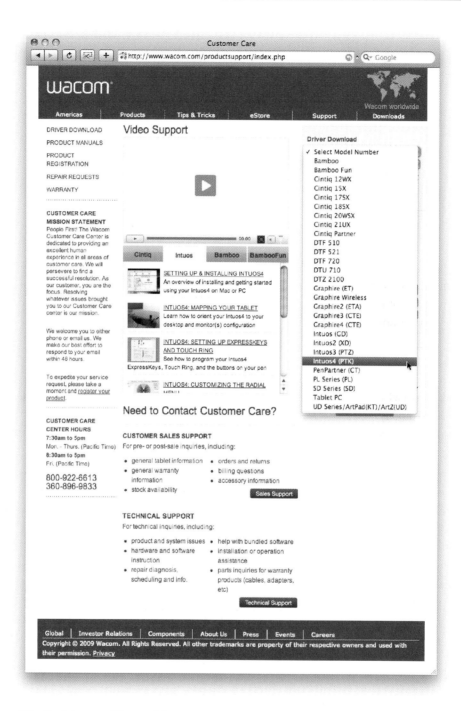

Figure 1.3 Update your Wacom driver.

Figure 1.4 The Wacom stroke nib.

5 Place your tablet in front of you, between you and your computer screen, either flat on your desk or on your lap, depending what is most comfortable for you. Your forearms should be able to rest comfortably on your tablet without you being hunched or needing to strain or stretch your arms or wrists in any way.

6 Orientate your Wacom Intuos4 so the ExpressKeys are on the same side as your non-favored hand (that is, on your left if you are right-handed, and vice versa).

7 Make sure the USB tablet cable is connected to the most convenient socket on your tablet and is tucked out of the way, not trailing over your keyboard. There are two alternative socket locations on the side of the tablet.

8 Hold your Wacom Grip Pen in a relaxed grip close to the tip and slightly more upright than you might hold a pencil.

9 Let the side of your hand that is gripping the Grip Pen rest gently on the surface of the tablet. This allows you to have full control of the pen pressure as you pivot your hand. This also gives you full control of the pen tip when you are holding it just above the tablet surface, allowing you to navigate anywhere on the screen without accidentally clicking or dragging. If you find your hand has too much resistance on the tablet surface due to sweat then try wearing a thin cotton photo glove with the fingers cut off.

10 Make a habit of getting up out of your chair at least every 15 to 20 minutes, even if only for a short walk around the room. Take the opportunity to breathe and gently stretch (be careful, always move gently and within your comfort zone). Besides the physical benefits, such mini-breaks help you get distance from your art and see things with a fresh perspective.

11 Keep hydrated. Drink plenty of water.

Elevating your laptop helps keep it cool, protects it from spills, places the screen at a more comfortable height and also opens up more space on your physical desktop. I use the Griffin elevator, which is suitable for Mac and PC laptops and is easily portable. See: http://www.griffintechnology. com/products/elevator

Wacom Control Panel Settings

Grip Pen

Before you open the Wacom control panel, first open Corel Painter 11. This will allow you to conveniently program Painter-specific Wacom settings. You can leave the Painter welcome screen up if you wish. On a Mac choose Corel Painter 11 > Hide Corel Painter 11. On a PC click the minimize application icon in the top right corner. You will be returning to Painter later.

On a Mac choose the apple menu > System Preferences and click on the Wacom icon in the very bottom section (Other) of the System Preferences. In Windows Vista go to the Start > Control Panel and left click on the Wacom Tablet Properties control panel icon. In Windows XP go to the Start > Settings > Control Panel and left click on the Wacom Tablet Properties (at bottom of list).

In the top half of the Wacom control panel you'll see the three horizontal panels labeled Tablet, Tool and Application. In the Tablet panel you'll see your current tablet highlighted, plus any other tablets listed that you have used with the same computer. In the Tool panel you'll see your current pen highlighted, plus any other pens listed (for example Grip Pen 1, Grip Pen 2). By double clicking on your pen icon names you can rename them so they are easily identifiable. This is useful if you have different pens assigned to different users.

In the Application panel you'll initially see one icon labeled "All." Click on the "+" box to the right of the Application panel and select Corel Painter 11 from the Currently Open Applications list. Click OK. You'll now see a Corel Painter 11 icon in the Application panel to the right of the original icon which now says "All Other." By selecting the Painter icon you will be

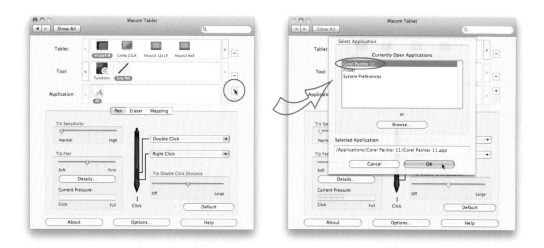

Figure 1.5 Add Corel Painter 11 to the Application panel.

able to make custom pen settings especially for working in Painter. You will know when an icon is selected since the selected icon and its title will be highlighted.

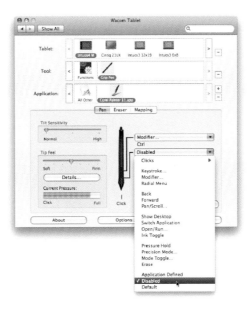

Figure 1.6 Setting the Grip Pen Two-Function button.

With the Grip Pen active in the Tools panel, Corel Painter 11 selected in the Application panel, and the Pen tab active (immediately below the Application panel and to the left of the Eraser and Mapping tabs), choose Disabled for the front function of the Two-Function pen button, and on the Mac choose Modifier with Control checked for the rear function, and on the PC Click > Right Click for the rear function. The disabled front function is to avoid accidentally choosing a command while painting. The Control (Mac)/Right Click (PC) command is useful for giving access to a fly out menu while your cursor is on the canvas in Painter that shows all the brush variants in the current category. Please note that these, and all other settings I share here, are simply my own personal preferences and should be treated only as a guide to try out. By setting the pen up with the Corel Painter 11 application selected you can have different Two-Function button settings for when you are working outside of Painter.

Mapping

Click on the Mapping tab. First ensure the Orientation setting matches what you need. If you are right-handed and require a horizontal orientation then the default ExpressKeys Left should be fine. If you're left-handed then choose ExpressKeys Right. The ExpressKeys Top and Bottom are for those who wish to work with their tablet vertically.

If you are working with a single display, leave the Screen Area: Full. This will ensure you have access to the entire screen from your tablet. If you have multiple monitors I recommend you choose one display in this setting and then set one of your ExpressKeys to Display Toggle, which alternates which display the tablet maps to, thus giving you full tablet mapping for each display.

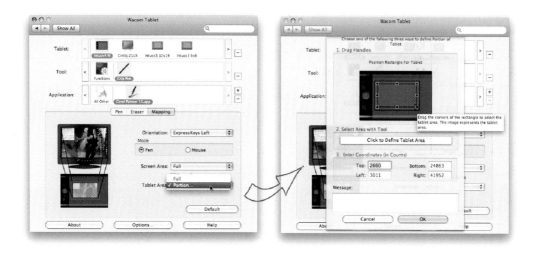

Figure 1.7 Adjust the tablet mapping from Full to Portion.

Change Tablet Area from Full to Portion. Use the top section called "1. Drag Handles" to define the portion of the tablet that is the active area. Drag the corners in from the edges at least a little. This prevents your pen tip from accidentally getting caught in the little "gulley" at the edge of the Full active surface on the tablet. If you have a Intuos4 L or XL (roughly equivalent to the old 9 × 12 and 12 × 19) then you may wish to keep the active area to a smaller portion of the tablet. Do whatever is comfortable. You can always change this setting anytime. Click OK when you have done this.

ExpressKeys

Click on the Functions icon in the Tools panel (it is positioned on the left of the panel). Again click on the " + " box to the right of the Applications panel and select Corel Painter 11 from the Currently Open Applications list.

You will see the ExpressKeys tab highlighted (to the left of the TouchRing and Radial Menu tabs). The ExpressKey settings I use in Painter are summarized below. There are eight ExpressKeys in total, four above the TouchRing and four below. In this summary I identify the ExpressKeys with numbers 1 through 8, 1 being the top ExpressKey and 8 being the bottom key.

ExpressKey (from top)	Function (if not specified Mac or PC, then assume it applies to both)	LED Label (type in for keystroke programming)
1	Keystroke: Shift-Cmd-S (Mac) / Shift-Ctrl-S (PC)	Save As
2	Radial Menu	Radial Menu
3	Keystroke: u	Clone Color
4	Keystroke: Cmd-M (Mac) / Ctrl-M (PC)	Screen Mode
5	Keystroke: Tab	Hide / Show Palettes
6	Modifier: Opt (Mac) / Alt (PC)	Opt (Mac) / Alt (PC)
7	Modifier: Opt + Cmd (Mac) / Alt + Ctrl (PC)	Opt + Cmd (Mac) / Alt + Ctrl (PC)
8	Keystroke: Space bar	Grabber Hand

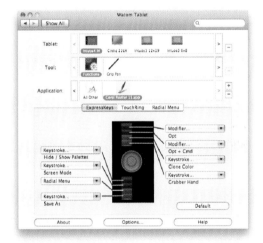

Figure 1.8 Suggested ExpressKeys settings.

When programming the Keystroke function, to clear an erroneous command you need to press the Clear button in the lower left of the Keystroke programming window. If you press the Delete key on your keyboard that will be registered as a programmed command, not as a way to undo what you've already typed in. Under the Keystrokes window, after setting the shortcut, you will be asked to name the ExpressKey shortcut. I suggest you use the same names as I have. The names you choose will then appear as a reminder on the LED display next to the corresponding ExpressKey.

Figure 1.9 An example of Keystroke programming.

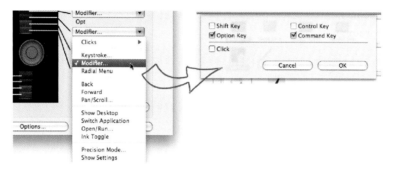

Figure 1.10 An example of Modifier programming.

The Radial Menu command leads to menus which are programmed in the Tool: Functions > Radial Menu tab section of the Wacom control panel. If you choose not to use Radial Menus you could use this ExpressKey for another function. I have not used all the possible functions available. For instance, I do not use the Precision Mode, which slows your cursor movement—a feature designed for those using a small tablet active area.

TouchRing

Click on the TouchRing tab. The TouchRing can be programmed to have up to four different functions which you toggle between by clicking on the round button in the center of the TouchRing. Make sure the Corel Painter 11 application is still selected in the Application panel since we are going to program a TouchRing setting just for use in Painter. I've chosen to keep things simple and have made the TouchRing a dedicated Zoom tool for zooming in and out of images open in Painter.

Radial Menu (Advanced)

Programming my Wacom Radial Menus for use in Painter is a complex and time-consuming operation. You do not need to program these menus with my settings in order to paint in Painter. If you are a beginner I recommend you omit this section and skip ahead to the next section *Installing Extra Brushes.*

Click on the Radial Menu tab, making sure you still have Corel Painter 11 active in the Application panel. Initially you will see the word "Top" highlighted in the left of the Radial Menu programming window. The "Top" represents the first Radial Menu you will see when you select the Radial Menu ExpressKey. Note that if you don't program an ExpressKey to be Radial Menu then you have no way to access the Radial Menus, even if you program them. You will initially see the default settings for the Top Radial Menu. For Painter I have completely customized the Radial Menus.

Leaving "Top" highlighted on the left, click on the top-most of the eight "pie"segments of the Top Radial Menu, pictorially represented in the center of the window. When you click on each segment it will become highlighted and you will be able to program and rename that particular segment. The programming is achieved through a drop down Function menu on the right. Almost every shortcut I have programmed uses the Keystroke function where, as with the ExpressKeys Keystroke programming, I program a keyboard shortcut and name the shortcut (that name will appear on the Radial Menu you see on your screen).

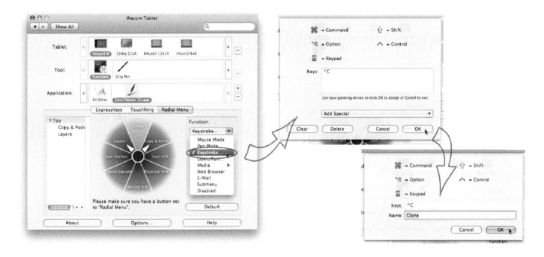

Figure 1.11 Programming a Radial Menu function using the Keystrokes option.

The only exceptions are the two segments you see with solid triangles pointing outwards (named "Layers" and "Copy & Paste"). These are both examples where I chose Function: Submenu instead of Function: Keystroke. The submenus lead to nested Radial Menus.

To program the shortcuts for the Radial Menus I had to go into Corel Painter 11 and customize some of the keyboard shortcuts within the program. I did this by accessing the Customize Keys Preferences within Painter: Corel Painter 11 > Preferences > Customize Keys (Mac)/Edit > Preferences > Customize Keys (PC). The Customize Keys custom shortcut settings are somewhat arbitrary and I have chosen them to avoid conflicts with existing default shortcuts. If you are a

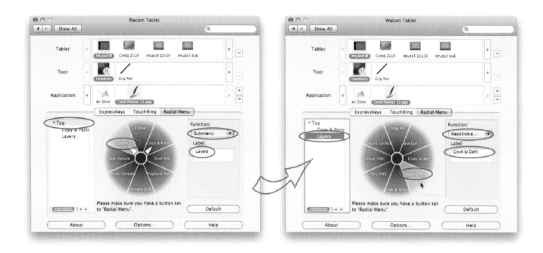

Figure 1.12 Programming a Radial Menu submenu.

member of PaintboxJ and have downloaded my Jeremy_P11_Workspace1 then you will already have most, if not all, of my custom Customize Keys Preferences already programmed in that workspace. Even if you have my workspace installed in Painter you would still need to manually program the Radial Menu settings in the Wacom control panel. As of the time of writing this book there is no way I am aware of how to automatically share Wacom settings in the same way that workspaces allow you to share custom settings in Painter.

Here are my Radial Menu settings, with segment 1 being the top-most segment, and then working around clockwise for segments 2, 3, 4, and so on. Where you see that I had to program the Customize Keys Preferences in Painter I have noted which of the Shortcut options I used (App. Menus for Application Menus, Plt. Menus for Palette Menus, etc.) and which Application commands I used within those menus (File, Edit, Selection, Brush Plt. for Brush Palette, etc.). The labels have been abbreviated to fit into the small amount of space available on each segment.

"Top" Radial Menu

Segment	Function (assume keystroke used unless the function is submenu)	Label	Had to program Customize Keys Preferences in Painter?
1	Ctrl-C (Mac)/C (PC)	Clone	Yes (App. Menu: File)
2	Submenu	Copy & Paste	
3	Shift-Cmd-S (Mac)/Shift-Alt-S (PC)	Save Strk	Yes (Plt. Menus: Brush Plt.)

(Continued)

(*Continued*)

Segment	Function (assume keystroke used unless the function is submenu)	Label	Had to program Customize Keys Preferences in Painter?
4	Shift-Cmd-P (Mac)/Shift-Alt-P (PC)	Playback Strk	Yes (Plt. Menus: Brush Plt.)
5	Shift-Cmd-R (Mac)/Shift-Alt-R (PC)	Record Strk	Yes (Plt. Menus: Brush Plt.)
6	Ctrl-Shift-R (Mac)/Shift-R (PC)	Reset Variant	Yes (Plt. Menus: Brush Plt.)
7	Ctrl-V (Mac)/Ctrl-J (PC)	Save Variant	Yes (Plt. Menus: Brush Plt.)
8	Submenu	Layers	

"Copy & Paste" Radial Submenu (click on "Copy & Paste" on the left side of the Radial Menus window)

Segment	Function (assume keystroke used unless the function is submenu)	Label	Had to Program Customize Keys (Application Menus) Preferences in Painter?
1	Cmd-C (Mac)/Ctrl-C (PC)	Copy	No (default)
2	Cmd-V (Mac)/Ctrl-V (PC)	Paste	Yes (App. Menu: Edit)
3	Shft-Cmd-V (Mac)/Shft-Ctrl-V (PC)	Paste in Place	Yes (App. Menu: Edit)
4	Opt-Cmd-V (Mac)/Alt-Ctrl-V (PC)	Paste in New	Yes (App. Menu: Edit)
5	Ctrl-S (Mac)/S (PC)	Stroke Slctn	Yes (App. Menu: Select)
6	Ctrl-F (Mac)/F (PC)	Float	Yes (App. Menu: Select)
7	Cmd-D (Mac)/Ctrl-D (PC)	Clear	No (default)
8	Cmd-A (Mac)/Ctrl-A (PC)	Select All	No (default)

"Layers" Radial Submenu (click on "Layers" on the left side of the Radial Menus window)

Segment	Function (assume keystroke used unless the function is submenu)	Label	Had to Program Customize Keys Preferences in Painter?
1	Opt-Ctrl-D (Mac)/Alt-D (PC)	Drop All	Yes (App. Menu: Layers)
2	Shift-Cmd-N (Mac)/Shift-Ctrl-N (PC)	New Lyr	No (default)
3	Shift-Cmd-R (Mac)/Ctrl-Alt-R (PC)	Conv to Ref	Yes (App. Menu: Layers)
4	Ctrl-D (Mac)/Ctrl-H (PC)	Cnvt to Deflt	Yes (Plt. Menu: Layers)
5	Shift-Opt-D (Mac)/Ctrl-Alt-D (PC)	Drop & Select	Yes (App. Menu: Layers)
6	Shift-Cmd-L (Mac)/Shift-Ctrl-L (PC)	Dry DWC	No (default)
7	Ctrl-Shift-D (Mac)/Shift-D (PC)	Diffuse DWC	Yes (App. Menu: Layers)
8	Shift-Ctrl-L (Mac and PC)	Create LyrMsk	Yes (App. Menu: Layers)

Install Extra Brushes

When you first install Corel Painter 11 the program already includes over 800 wonderful and diverse brushes (which you will see summarized in the next chapter). In that case why bother to install even more brushes? You can certainly create beautiful paintings with just the default brushes. The answer lies in the power of expanding your range of creative possibilities. You may not use the extra brushes in every painting, but now and then you will be able to achieve a look or effect that you wouldn't have otherwise had at your fingertips.

My motivation for installing extra brushes started when I found that some of my old favorite brushes from earlier versions of Painter, such as "Modern Art in a Can" and "Big Wet Luscious," were dropped from the default install of later versions of the program. I also found, as I tweaked and played with the characteristics of my favorite brushes, such as the Sargent Brush, that I created new custom brushes such as "Jeremy's MishMashScumble" and "Jeremy's SumiPollock Splash" that I wanted to reuse repeatedly. Finally, friends of mine kindly allowed me to share some of their own great custom brushes, such as the acclaimed "Den's Oil Funky Chunky" by Denise Laurent (see the contributors list). Once you have used these extra brushes you won't want to be without them in your brush library.

With or without extra brushes, the large number of brushes can be overwhelming. To help you cope with so many individual brushes, which are known in Painter as "variants," they are divided into groupings of similar brushes, or brush types. These groupings are known as "categories." The categories themselves are grouped together into a brush "library." The default brush library in Painter is called "Painter Brushes." Thus the hierarchy is library > categories > variants. This hierarchy is reflected in the physical folder hierarchy on your computer hard drive:

Applications > Corel Painter 11 > Brushes > Painter Brushes (the default brush library folder) > category folders and icons > variants (Mac).

Local Disc (C:) > Program Files > Corel > Corel Painter 11 > Brushes > Painter Brushes (the default brush library folder) > category folders and icons > variants (PC).

When you understand this hierarchy then installing extra brushes is easy. You have to be aware of whether you are installing a brush library or a brush category (which comprises a folder accompanied by a 30 pixel by 30 pixel icon jpg of the same name) or individual variant files. You then copy the items into the right location in the hierarchy of folders. Brush categories will be copied into the Painter Brushes library folder (*not* into the Brushes folder—a common mistake).

The Resource Disc (CD-ROM) that comes with this book includes a brush category called "JeremyFaves2." This category contains a mix of golden oldie brushes from earlier versions of Painter and custom brushes created by myself and others. To install the JeremyFaves2 brush category follow these instructions.

Installing the JeremyFaves2 brush category on a Mac:

1 Place the Resource Disc in your computer.

2 In the Macintosh Finder, double click on the Resource Disc icon on your desktop.

3 Double click on the Extra Brush Category folder. You will now see a JeremyFaves2 folder and JeremyFaves2.jpg image file.

4 Drag the the Extra Brush Category window by the top title bar to the right side of your screen.

5 Double click on your hard drive icon on your desktop.

6 Select Applications in the Finder browser sidebar.

7 Select Corel Painter 11 > Brushes > Painter Brushes. You will see a long list of category folders and their icons (Acrylics, Airbrushes, etc.).

8 Place the Painter Brushes window on the left side of your screen.

9 Select both the JeremyFaves2 folder and JeremyFaves2.jpg image file (hold the Shift key down as you click on each of them in turn, or drag your cursor across them both).

Drag the JeremyFaves2 folder and JeremyFaves2.jpg icon into Applications > Corel Painter 11 > Brushes > Painter Brushes folder.

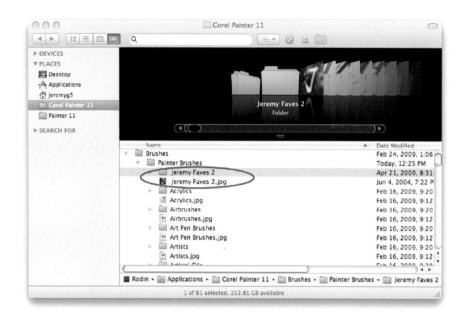

Figure 1.13 This is what you should see on your hard drive when you have successfully copied the JeremyFaves2 category folder and jpg into the Painter Brushes folder (Mac).

Installing the JeremyFaves2 brush category on a PC:

1 Place the Resource Disc in your computer.
2 In My Computer (Windows XP) or Windows Explorer (Windows Vista), locate the Resource Disc, which is usually on the CD Drive (D:).
3 Open the Resource Disc > Extra Brush Category folder so you see a JeremyFaves2 folder and JeremyFaves2.jpg image file.

Select both the JeremyFaves2 folder and JeremyFaves2.jpg image file (hold the Ctrl key down as you click on each of them in turn, or drag your cursor across them both).

Figure 1.14 Select the JeremyFaves2 category folder and jpg (PC).

1 Choose Edit > Copy to Folder. A "Copy Items" browsing window will pop up in which you can locate the folder to which you wish to copy the selected items.

In the "Copy Items" browsing window choose Local Disc (C:) > Program Files > Corel > Corel Painter 11 > Brushes > Painter Brushes. You will see a long list of category folders and their icons (Acrylics, Airbrushes, etc.).

2   Click on Copy.

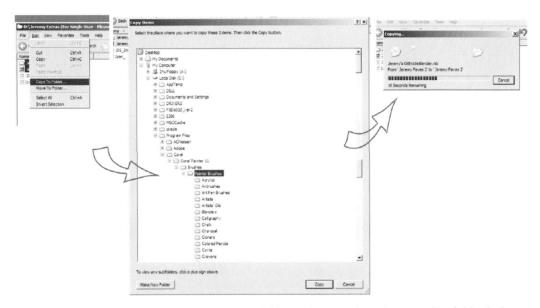

Figure 1.15   Copy the JeremyFaves2 category folder and jpg to the Painter Brushes folder (PC).

To make sure your brush installation has been successful, open Painter. If it is already open then click on the small solid black triangle in the upper right corner of the Brush Selector palette. You'll see the Brush Selector pop-up menu. Choose Load Brush Library. You'll see the Painter Brushes library selected in the Brush Library window. Choose Load. You'll now see the JeremyFaves2 category appear in the bottom of the brush category list. This applies to Mac or PC. If Painter is not open then just open Painter to check if the new brush category is visible in the Brush Selector. The brush library is automatically updated when you open Painter so you don't need to reload the brush library.

Brushes are the most position-critical items you will have to install. If they are copied into the wrong level of the hierarchy, or if you do not take them out of the Extra Brush Category folder, they will not work. The two most common mistakes are copying them into the Brushes folder, which is the location for brush libraries, not categories, or leaving them in the Extra Brush Category folder they are contained in on the Resource Disc. In either of these cases the brushes will not work. If you run into problems, please reread the instructions above very carefully. Please also look carefully at the accompanying figures showing you what you should see in your Painter Brushes folder.

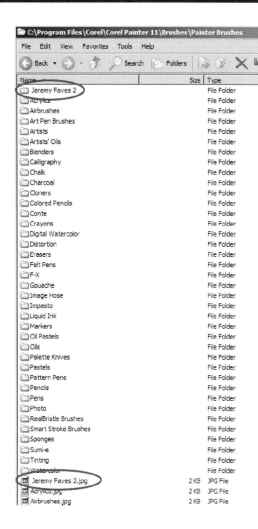

Figure 1.16 This is what you should see on your hard drive when you have successfully copied the JeremyFaves2 category folder and jpg into the Painter Brushes directory (PC).

If you already have the JeremyFaves2 category from earlier versions of this book then you do not need to install it again. If you have the JeremyOwnFaves4 and JeremyGuestfaves4 categories from my DVD *How to Paint from Photographs Using Corel Painter X* then install those categories *instead* of JeremyFaves2, since every brush in JeremyFaves2 is already part of that larger set of brushes. The JeremyBoxSet1 brush category, available to members of PaintboxJ.com, is a completely new set of custom brushes that are not included in any other set. Follow the same procedures for installing any of these other brush categories.

Install Extra Art Materials

"Art Materials" in the context of Painter refers to such items as Color Sets, Nozzles, Papers, Patterns, etc. Painter comes with default libraries of all these art materials, so you do not need to

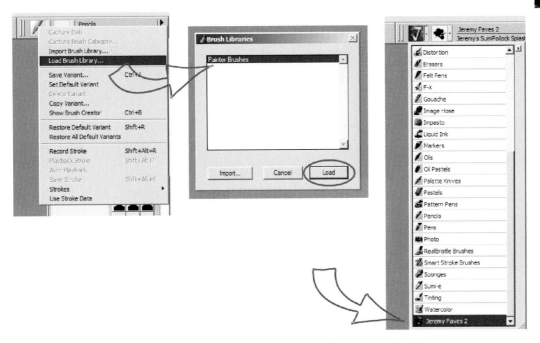

Figure 1.17 How to load a newly installed brush category if Painter is already open.

add extra libraries in order to paint. However, as with brushes, there is power in expanding the diversity of mark-making capabilities you have at your fingertips. For this reason I recommend taking advantage of the opportunity to install the extra art materials provided in the Resource Disc that comes with this book. Unlike brushes, art materials are not location sensitive. They can be placed anywhere and loaded into Painter from anywhere. For convenience I recommend storing them in the Corel Painter 11 > Support Files folder. Here are the steps for installing the extra art materials.

Installing extra art materials on a Mac:

1 Place the Resource Disc in your computer.
2 In the Macintosh Finder, double click on the Resource Disc icon on your desktop.
3 Double click on the Extra Art Materials folder. You will now see three items: JeremyFaveNozzles1, JeremyFavePapers2 and JeremyFavePtrns2.
4 Drag the the Extra Art Materials window by the top title bar to the right side of your screen.
5 Double click on your hard drive icon on your desktop.
6 Select Applications in the Finder browser sidebar.
7 Select Corel Painter 11 > Support Files. You will see three folders: Color Sets, Plugins and Templates.
8 Place the Support Files window on the left side of your screen.

9 Returning to the Extra Art Materials window on the right, select the three items JeremyFaveNozzles1, JeremyFavePapers2 and JeremyFavePtrns2 (hold the Shift key down as you click on each of them in turn, or drag your cursor across them all).

10 Drag the three selected items into the Applications > Corel Painter 11 > Support Files folder.

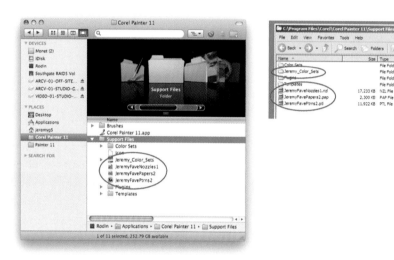

Figure 1.18 This is what you should see when you have successfully copied the extra art materials into the Support Files folder.

Installing extra art materials on a PC:

1 Place the Resource Disc in your computer.

2 In My Computer (Windows XP) or Windows Explorer (Windows Vista), locate the Resource Disc, which is usually on the CD Drive (D:).

3 Open the Resource Disc > Extra Art Materials folder so you see JeremyFaveNozzles1, JeremyFavePapers2 and JeremyFavePtrns2.

4 Select JeremyFaveNozzles1, JeremyFavePapers2 and JeremyFavePtrns2 (hold the Ctrl key down as you click on each of them in turn, or drag your cursor across them both).

5 Choose Edit > Copy to Folder. A Copy Items browsing window will pop up in which you can locate the folder you to which wish to copy the selected items.

6 In the Copy Items browsing window choose Local Disc (C:) > Program Files > Corel > Corel Painter 11 > Support Files.

7 Click on Copy.

Install Extra Workspaces

A "workspace" in Painter is the entire collection of custom data that uniquely defines every aspect of the Painter interface, including what art material libraries are loaded, the content order of each of those libraries, the brush categories and variants that you see, the custom palettes, the palette arrangements, and so on. A Painter workspace is much more than just the palette arrangements. This can be a little confusing at first. It is easy to accidentally generate new workspaces instead of saving new palette arrangements.

When you install Painter you are automatically in the default workspace, which is called "Default." You can do everything fine in the default workspace. However, by importing a custom workspace, in an instant you can experience a completely customized Painter interface that may have taken someone else many hours of trial and error to develop and make. This is the case with my "Jeremy_P11C_Workspace.pws" that is included on the Resource Disc that comes with this book and with my "Jeremy_P11_Workspace1.pws" that I share on PaintboxJ. Thus the value of importing a custom workspace is the convenience and the time saved.

If you wish to install a custom workspace (a file which will have a name ending in ".pws") use the Window > Workspace > Import Workspace menu command in Painter. If you install the workspace "Jeremy_P11C_Workspace.pws" that is included in the Resource Disc that comes with this book, or are a PaintboxJ member and have installed the "Jeremy_P11_Workspace1.pws" then you do not need to do the set up described below since that is all included in the custom workspace.

Whenever you close Painter, the state that you leave the current workspace in will be remembered when you next open Painter. In other words you don't need to worry about saving or updating your current workspace, Painter does that automatically. If you end up customizing the current workspace to the extent that you'd like to preserve it and be able to use it on other computers, then simply choose Window > Workspace > Export Workspace. This will generate a custom workspace file of a name of your choosing (with the ending ".pws"), saved anywhere you wish to save it, that you can then import into Painter on another computer. The remainder of this book assumes you are working with the Default workspace.

Install Extra Templates

If you are reusing the same image, or size of canvas, again and again in different projects and sessions, then the Templates feature can be very useful. The Templates feature of Painter allows you to have quick access (via a welcome screen pop-up menu or the File > Open Template command) to any Painter RIFF format image file saved in the Applications/Program Files > Corel Painter 11 > Support Files > Templates folder. To load in a non-RIFF image as a template, open it in Painter and then save it as a Painter RIFF file in the Templates folder. If the file or files are already Painter RIFF files just copy them into the Templates folder. You will find some standard size canvases already saved as RIFFs, available to add to the Templates folder, on PaintboxJ.com.

Set Up Corel Painter 11

Check for Updates

I recommend you regularly check the url: http://www.corel.com/painter for Painter patches and updates, and always ensure you have the most up-to-date version of Painter.

Figure 1.19 The Corel web site—a great resource for Painter tutorials, training, links and updates.

Welcome Screen

1 Open Corel Painter 11, or make the program active if it is already open on your computer.
2 You will initially see a welcome screen with a Painter artwork sample that you can change by clicking on the small circular arrow icon directly below the artwork image.

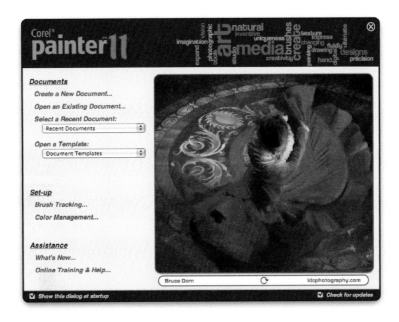

Figure 1.20 The Corel Painter 11 welcome screen.

3 Close the welcome screen by clicking on the Close button in the top right corner of the window.

4 Choose Help > Welcome and you will see the welcome screen reappear.

5 Under Assistance in the welcome screen, click on What's New. You'll see a summary of all the new features in Painter 11.

6 Return to the welcome screen and click on Online Training & Help, also under Assistance. This link leads you to a web page full of useful links and resources. An alternative route to this page is via the Help > Tutorials menu.

7 Close the welcome screen.

8 Choose Help > User Guide. This will open a 54 page PDF Corel Painter 11 User Guide.

Color Management

1 Choose Help > Corel Painter 11 Help (Mac) or Help > Help Topics > Search tab (PC). The searchable Painter 11 Help is an immensely useful resource in Painter and one I recommend taking full advantage of.

2 Write in "understanding color management" in the search field and select the page of that title. Read the article—an easy-to-read, concise introduction to color management. Color management is the art of getting color consistency, accuracy and repeatability throughout your workflow. It is a complex topic beyond the scope of this book. There are many excellent books, DVDs, online resources, classes and workshops devoted to the subject.

The Painter Color Management settings I use are as follows:

3 Choose Canvas > Color Management Settings, also accessible from the Color Management link in the welcome screen or via the keyboard shortcut Opt-Cmd-K (Mac)/Alt-Ctrl-K (PC).

4 Change the Default Color Profile from sRGB IEC61966-2-1 to Adobe RGB (1998), a larger color space. Using this default profile you will find that your images open in Painter match closer to the same images open in Photoshop.

5 Choose Canvas > Color Proofing Settings.

6 Set the Simulate Device option also to Adobe RGB (1998).

New Canvas

When you open a new digital canvas in Painter you can determine the width and height of the image either in number of pixels, or in units of length (inches, cm, etc.). If you set the width and length in pixels, the Resolution setting (pixels per inch, PPI or ppi) can be any number without affecting the number of pixels in the image. If you set the width and height in inches (or any other unit of length) then the Resolution (ppi) setting determines how many pixels will be in your image. Within Painter you will be setting ppi, not dpi (dots per inch, DPI or dpi).

1 Choose File > New or keyboard shortcut Cmd-N (Mac)/Ctrl-N (PC).

2 In the New Image dialog window set the width and height units to inches.

3 Set the width to 16 inches and the height to 11 inches.

4 Set the Resolution to 200 pixels per inch.

5 Leave Paper Color white and Picture Type: Image.

6 Click OK.

7 Choose Window > Screen Mode Toggle or use the keyboard shortcut Cmd-M (Mac)/Ctrl-M (PC). This command is near the bottom of the Window menu. It will mount your canvas on your screen.

Figure 1.21 Open a new canvas.

PPI Versus DPI?

Terminology in digital painting can get a little confusing. This is especially the case when it comes to distinguishing between the units of resolution—pixels per inch (PPI or ppi) and dots per inch (DPI or dpi)—and between the resolution of a digital file and of a computer screen.

Let's start with the basics. Computers are binary digit calculating machines. Everything they do is based on digital data made up of "on" and "off" states—ones and zeros—known as "bits," a name derived from "Binary digITs." Packets of this digital data define the digital images you paint in Painter. These packets of data define the visual characteristics (hue, value and intensity) of each picture element, known as a "pixel," in an array or grid of pixels that are spread out like a chessboard. This data can be translated by an output device into a visible array of picture elements, such as pixels on a computer screen or dots on a printed surface, which our visual perception system very successfully interprets as a continuous, smooth image.

The pixel resolution of a digital image file (measured in pixels per inch) multiplied by the width (measured in inches) will always equal the numbers of pixels across the width of the image, and similarly for the height.

A computer screen displays a number of pixels wide by number of pixels high (e.g. 1024 × 768), at a fixed pixel resolution (e.g. 72 pixels per inch). These numbers are *not* related to the number of pixels wide by number of pixels high, and the pixel resolution, of your digital image. The computer screen can display your image zoomed in, in which case several computer screen pixels may represent each pixel in your digital file, or zoomed out, in which case each computer screen pixel may represent many pixels in your image.

When your image pixel data are used by a printer to create a visible array of dots on a substrate like paper or canvas, the resolution of those dots is measured in units of dots per inch (DPI or dpi).

Default Palette Arrangement

Choose Window > Palette Arrangement > Default. You'll now see the default palette arrangement for Painter, which is the same as the arrangement you see when you first install Painter. You will always be able to return to this arrangement anytime by selecting the same Window > Palette Arrangement > Default command.

Brush Tracking

1 Locate the Brush Selector palette in the upper right of your screen.
2 Click on the left-most icon of the two icons in the Brush Selector palette. You will see a pop-up menu which lists all the brush categories in the current brush library.
3 Choose the Artist category.
4 Click on the right-most icon of the two icons in the Brush Selector palette. You will see a pop-up menu which lists all the brush variants in the current brush category.
5 Click on Sargent Brush.
6 Set the Size slider setting in the Property Bar at the top of your screen to just over 50.

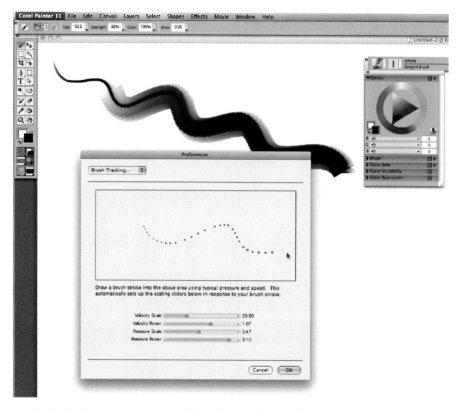

Figure 1.22 Calibrate your pen pressure in Painter using Brush Tracking.

7 Drag the cursor in the Saturation/Value Triangle of the Color palette (on the right of your screen, just below the Brush Selector palette) down to the lower left corner so you are painting with black.

8 Make a long undulating snake-like brush stroke across your canvas, starting off with very light pen pressure and gradually increasing the pressure. You will see the stroke get thicker with increasing pressure. If you do not get a smooth, well-controlled increase in thickness as you vary pressure, choose Corel Painter 11 > Preferences > Brush Tracking (Mac) or Edit > Preferences > Brush Tracking (PC), or use the keyboard shortcut Cmd-Shift-K (Mac)/Ctrl-Shift-K (PC).

9 Make a single light brush stroke across the scratchpad surface in the Brush Tracking window.

10 Click OK.

11 Now make another stroke and see if you have better control over the brush size as you vary the pressure. Continue this process until you are satisfied with the pressure-size control.

12 To clear your canvas choose Select > All or Cmd-A (Mac)/Ctrl-A (PC), followed by Delete (Mac) or Backspace (PC).

Brush Size

1 Choose Window > Brush Controls > Size. You will see a Size listed on a pop-out menu amongst a long set of Brush Controls palettes. If there is no check mark by Size that means it is currently hidden. In that case select Size in the pop-out menu.

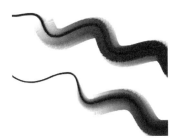

Figure 1.23 Before (top stroke) and after (bottom stroke) Brush Tracking.

2 You will now see the Size palette on your Painter desktop, along with a large number of closed Brush Controls palettes.

3 Drag the Size palette title bar and place it just above the General title bar at the top of the Brush Controls palettes. If you inadvertently drag the Size palette out of the Brush Controls palettes you can just drag it back in again.

4 If you minimized the Brush Size palette click on the left palette arrow in the Size palette bar and open it again.

5 Drag the lower right corner of the Brush Controls palettes upwards until you just see the Size slider and preview.

6 Grab the light gray title bar at the top of the Brush Controls palettes and drag the Brush Size palette into the lower right corner of your screen. This palette now gives you a convenient graphic indication of brush size at any time.

7 Change the Brush Size slider in the Brush Size palette and make a brush stroke.

8 Hold down the key combination Option-Cmd/Ctrl-Alt and click and drag in your canvas. As you drag your cursor you'll see a circle that represents your brush size. When you lift your pen from the tablet the brush size will be whatever the circle diameter was at that moment. This is the shortcut for changing brush size "on the fly" as you paint. If you programmed the shortcut into your Wacom Tablet ExpressKeys try it out at this time.

Brush Cursor

There are three ways that your brush cursor can be represented on your canvas. Choosing between these is a matter of personal preference. I recommend you initially try them all out.

If you're not sure which to use, then stick with the default Enhanced Brush Ghost. I personally like to see exactly where my brush stroke is starting and generally use the Drawing Cursor.

Enhanced Brush Ghost

The default representation method is the "Enhanced Brush Ghost" which depicts a faint circle whose diameter indicates the maximum brush diameter and whose center is where your brush stroke will begin. There is a "stick" that pivots in the center of the circle and indicates the bearing and tilt of your pen. If you are using the Wacom Art Pen then you will also see a small dot on the diameter circle that indicates rotation.

Enable Brush Ghosting

1 Choose Corel Painter 11 > Preferences > General (Mac) or Edit > Preferences > General (PC) or use keyboard shortcut Cmd-K (Mac)/Ctrl-K (PC).
2 Uncheck the "Enhanced Brush Ghost" checkbox, leaving the "Enable Brush Ghosting" checkbox checked.
3 Click OK. Note that now when you paint with the Artists > Sargent Brush you'll see a vertical rectangle shape until you start your brush stroke, at which time the brush tip position is represented by the Drawing Cursor.
4 Change the brush variant from Artists > Sargent Brush to Artists > Impressionist. Note the different shape of the brush ghost.
5 Change brush size and observe how the brush ghost reflects the new size.

Drawing Cursor

1 Choose Corel Painter 11 > Preferences > General (Mac) or Edit > Preferences > General (PC) or use keyboard shortcut Cmd-K (Mac)/Ctrl-K (PC).
2 Uncheck the "Enable Brush Ghosting" checkbox. Set the Drawing Cursor (represented by a small brush symbol or by other options accessible in the cursor pop up menu) direction to suit your handedness (towards upper left if you are right-handed and towards upper right if you are left-handed).
3 Click OK. This representation doesn't change with brush size or shape, and remains the same before, during and after the making of a brush stroke.

Other General Preferences Suggestions

1 Choose Corel Painter 11 > Preferences > General (Mac) or Edit > Preferences > General (PC) or use keyboard shortcut Cmd-K (Mac)/Ctrl-K (PC).

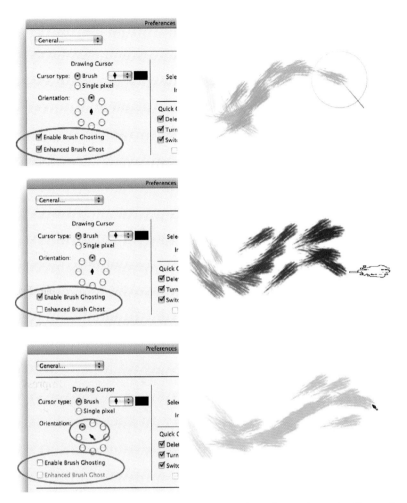

Figure 1.24 The three cursor options (top to bottom): Enhanced Brush Ghost, Enable Brush Ghosting and Drawing Cursor. Brush used for sample is the Artists: Impressionist.

2 Set Units to be inches. This sets the default units used for width and height in the New canvas and Resize dialog windows.

3 Uncheck "Create Backup on Save." Backup on Save is a useful feature if you do lots of Saves since it automatically saves a backup of the last saved state of your file. The backup files have file names ending in "_bak." In my workflow I use Save As rather than Save and therefore do not have a need for the backups.

4 Check "Draw Zoomed-out Views Using Area-Averaging" for faster screen draw.

5 Check "Display Warning When Drawing Outside Selection" since that it is a useful reminder on the occasions you overlook to deselect a selection.

Customize Keys

In the Customize Keys preference you can view the pre-assigned shortcuts and modify them if you wish, creating your own customized key sets. I recommend two modifications to the default shortcuts that avoid accidentally choosing the Brush Line command or Scissors tool when pasting or undoing.

1 If you are in the General Preferences window choose Customize Keys from the Preferences pop-up menu. Otherwise choose Corel Painter 11 > Preferences > Customize Keys (Mac) or Edit > Preferences > Customize Keys (PC).
2 Choose Shortcuts: Tools.
3 Click on the application command Brush Line which highlights the shortcut "V."
4 Choose Shift-V on your keyboard. This resets the default shortcut.
5 Scroll down to the application command Scissors which highlights the shortcut "Z."
6 Choose Shift-Z on your keyboard. This resets the default shortcut.

Please refer back to the section above that describes how I program the Wacom Intuos4 ExpressKeys for an extensive set of customized keystrokes that I program in using the Customize Keys preference.

Custom Palettes

Custom palettes are a great aid to efficient workflow. Painter offers you the ability to easily create, edit, export and import custom palettes containing convenient shortcuts for menu commands and brush variants. Besides being more efficient than navigating through drop down menus, custom palettes are also a great way to enhance your Painter workflow by grouping frequently used sequences of command and brush shortcuts next to one another.

1 Choose Window > Custom Palette > Add Command.
2 Choose File > Save As. Use menus, *not* keyboard shortcuts, when programming a command to add to a custom palette.
3 Choose OK. You will see a new custom palette appear containing just a Save As button. The custom palette title will be something generic like "Custom 1."
4 Choose Window > Custom Palette > Organizer.
5 Click on the name of the custom palette corresponding to the one you have just created.
6 Choose Rename.
7 Rename the custom palette with a meaningful name such as "Basic Shortcuts" (you can always rename it again later).
8 If you see other custom palettes that you wish to delete, select them all. If there is more than one you wish to delete use Cmd/Ctrl to select them individually or the Shift key to select a block of them. Then choose Delete.

9   Choose Done.

10   Choose Window > Custom Palette > Add Command.

11   Choose your custom palette name from the Add To pop-up menu.

12   Choose File > Clone.

13   Choose OK. You'll now see a Clone button added to your custom palette.

14   Repeat steps 10 through 13 for all the other menu command shortcuts you wish to add to your custom palette. You can make shortcuts for almost any menu command anywhere in Painter.

15   Choose a favorite brush in the Brush Selector palette, such as Artists > Sargent.

16   Drag either the category or variant icon from the Brush Selector palette into your custom palette. You will see the category icon appear in the custom palette as a shortcut to the particular variant.

17   You can repeat this for any other variants you like. However, if you pick more than one variant from the same category the shortcut icon will look the same, and there is no way to tell which shortcut is which other than memorizing the position or trying each one out.

Tracker Palette

The plus side of the Tracker is that it is a handy way to keep a record of the variants you use in a session, and allows you to store and access your favorite brushes. The down side is that it takes up a lot of space in your precious Painter desktop real estate. It can also be slow to load when full of variants. For these reasons I prefer to use the variant shortcuts in my custom palette. Try it out and decide for yourself if it works for you.

Choose Window > Show Tracker. You'll see a list of brush stroke dabs you have used in Painter. Resize the palette by dragging in the bottom right corner. Choose List from the Tracker pop-up menu (top right corner of the Tracker palette) so you see the names of the variants listed. Each time you use a new brush, the variant is saved on the Tracker palette—up to a maximum of 25 variants. You can return to a brush variant you like by choosing it from the Tracker palette. You can lock your favorite variants, so that they are always at the top of the Tracker palette, by selecting the variant in the Tracker and then clicking on the lock icon (lower left). Clicking again on the lock icon will unlock the variant. To clear selected (or all) unlocked brush variants choose Clear Selected (or Clear All) from the Tracker pop-up menu. Brush variants are stored in the Tracker after the document you were working on has been closed and between Corel Painter sessions.

Palette Layout

Palette layouts are a powerful tool for efficient workflow. You can save numerous different layouts for different tasks.

Figure 1.25 A basic palette layout.

Once you have settled on a palette layout you can save it:

1 Choose Window > Arrange Palettes > Save Layout.
2 Name your layout (such as "Basic").
3 Click OK. You will now see your saved layout listed under the Window > Arrange Palettes menu (Figure 1.26), unless there are already 16 palette layouts which is the maximum. If you reach the maximum you will need to choose Window > Arrange Palettes > Delete Layout and delete some of the layouts.

Figure 1.26 Saving a basic palette layout.

Congratulations on getting ready for action! Now you've got through the set up and preparation it's finally time to get painting…

Brush Guide

As you will already have discovered, one of the biggest challenges facing any user of Painter is the vast array of choices and options at almost every corner, whether it is the palettes and sub-palettes, menus and submenus, pop-ups within pop-ups, and so on. It can be overwhelming. Nowhere in the program is the abundance of riches more apparent than in the choice of brushes.

Brushes are the heart and soul of Painter. Back in the early 1990s Painter's creators, Mark Zimmer and the late (and sadly missed) Tom Hedges, worked tirelessly to create a wonderful collection of brushes that emulated the effects of painting and drawing in "natural media" (a term adopted by Fractal Design from the outset to describe non-digital art media).

Even with the grouping of brushes into categories, the challenge still remains of knowing which brush to choose to get a particular effect in your painting and trying to remember what each brush looks like. It can take a long time to go through every variant and try them all out, and by the time you finish you may have forgotten what the earlier variants look like! This Brush Guide is designed for quick reference to help set you in the right direction in your search for a particular brush look. Each figure in this glossary shows the look of every default variant contained within that category. The horizontal example brush strokes of each variant are arranged in the same vertical order that the variants appear listed in the Brush Selector variant pop-up

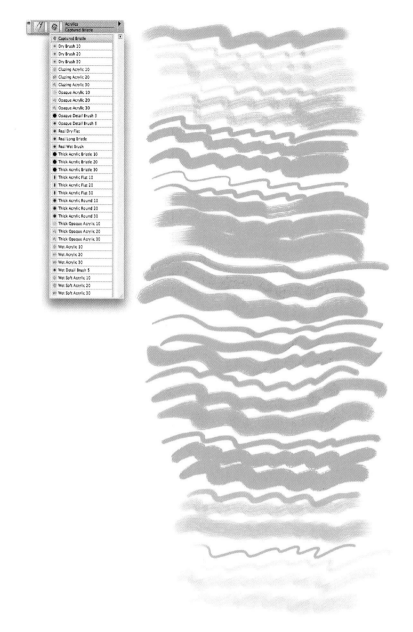

Figure 2.1 *Acrylics*—Try the Captured Bristle variant with Resat set to about 10% for a nice oily blender.

menu shown in each figure. Vertical strokes are included where they are needed to illustrate the blending, distorting, color mixing or erasing property of brushes.

I suggest you familiarize yourself with this guide and try out the brushes that I mention in the captions. Then return to it later, as needed.

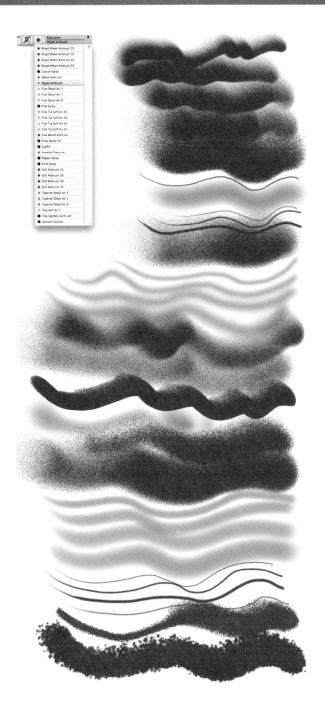

Figure 2.2 *Airbrushes*—The soft edged Digital Airbrush is my favorite brush variant for editing layer masks (using black to make layer transparent, and white to bring back layer opacity).

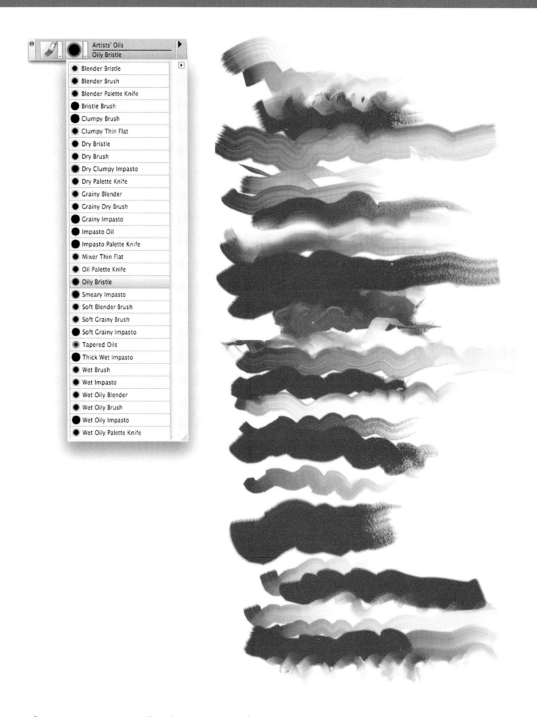

Figure 2.3 *Artists' Oils*—The Bristle Brush variant, used with the Mixer Pad's Sample Multiple Colors dropper, is great for short dab brush strokes.

Figure 2.4 *Artist*—You can't go wrong with the Sargent and Impressionist variants.

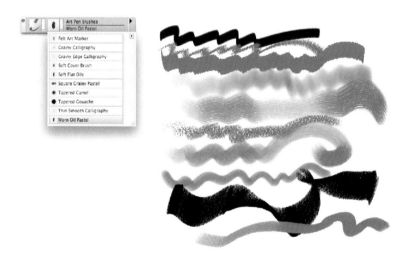

Figure 2.5 *Art Pen*—If you have a 6D Art Pen try it with the Thin Smooth Calligraphy brush variant and rotate the pen as you paint for some cool brush stroke variations.

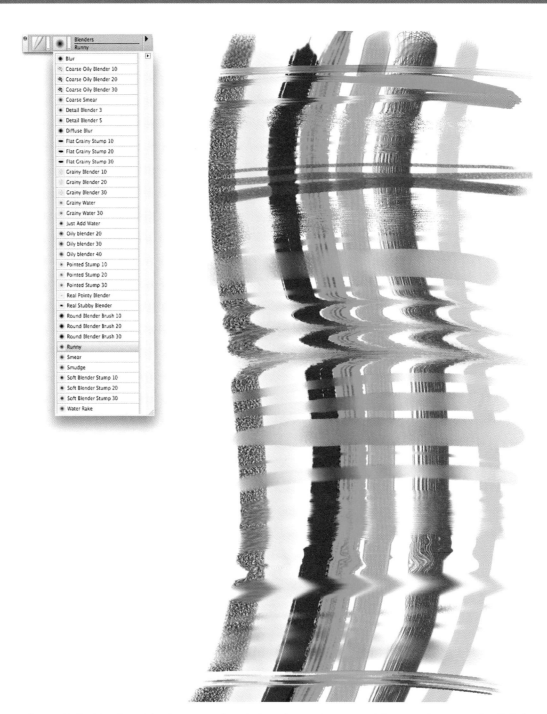

Figure 2.6 *Blenders*—The Runny variant is just the tool you need for creating smooth, slightly distorted oily edges.

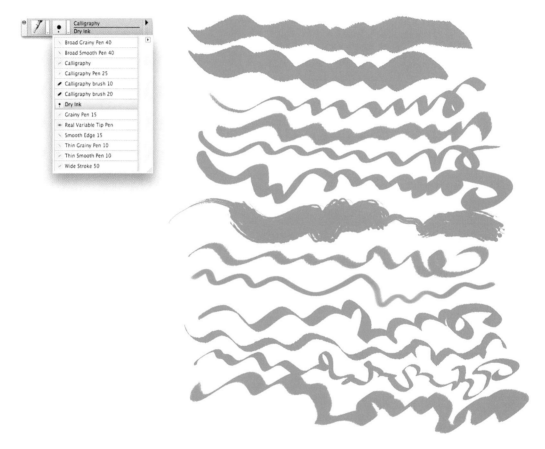

Figure 2.7 *Calligraphy*—For your calligraphic italicized signature try the Thin Smooth Pen 10, and for looser Zen calligraphy style brushwork try the Dry Ink.

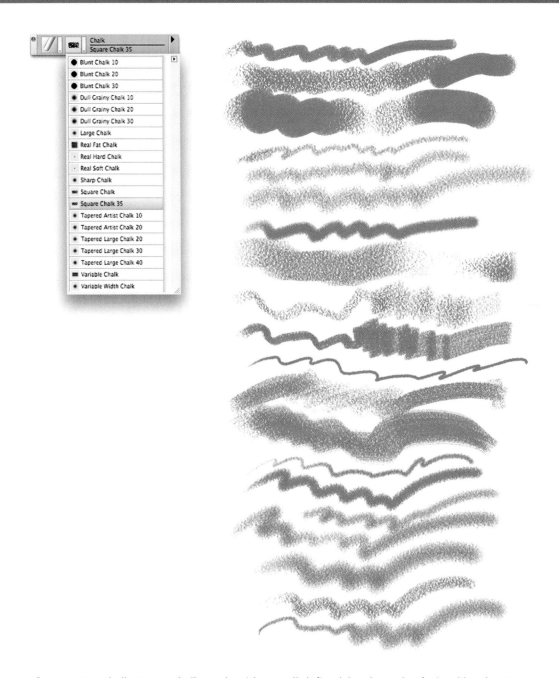

Figure 2.8 *Chalk*—For a chalk mark with a well-defined brush stroke feel, I like the Square Chalk 35, and for covering a lot of canvas without distinct brush marks, try the Real Fat Chalk.

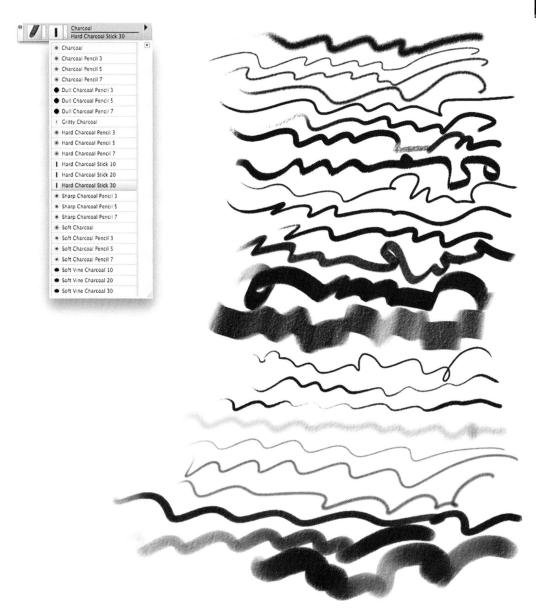

Figure 2.9 *Charcoal*—The Soft Charcoal Pencil 5 variant makes a very nice general drawing pencil.

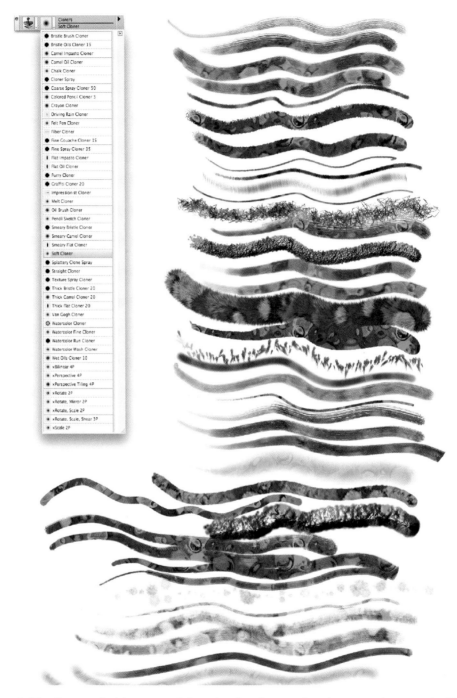

Figure 2.10 *Cloners*—A rich source of clone brushes for transforming your photographs. Try out the Smeary Camel Cloner for a classic oil look, and the Soft Cloner for bringing in an earlier stage of a painting into a later stage.

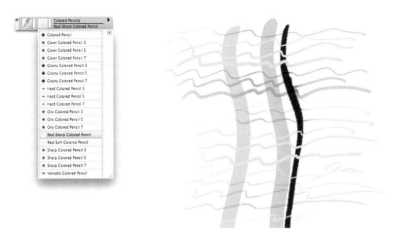

Figure 2.11 *Colored Pencils*—Notice how the Oily Colored Pencil 7 picks up color from where the stroke starts, making it good for short brush strokes.

Figure 2.12 *Conte*—I like the quality of the Real Soft Conte marks, and the way the Real Soft Conte variant reacts to the stylus tilt (it is an example of a new Hard Media brush).

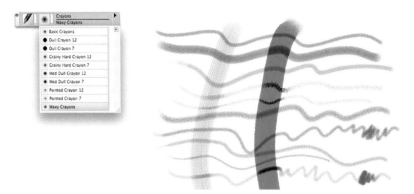

Figure 2.13 *Crayons*—The Pointed Crayon 12 is a good sketching tool. Be aware it is a build-up method variant and therefore is semi-translucent and does not cover up darker colors.

Figure 2.14 *Digital Watercolor*—Great for glazes. Try the Broad Water Brush to cover large areas quickly, the Diffuse Water for a soft soak-into-blotting paper edge and the Salt to spatter light spots. Note that Digital Watercolors act as if in a layer, even though not listed in the Layers list, and can be flattened by choosing Layers > Dry Digital Watercolor.

Figure 2.15 *Distortion*—These brushes primarily move paint that is already on the canvas. Confusion and Turbulence are both great for roughening up edges. Pinch and Distorto are good for defining boundaries, shapes and forms within a solid mass of colored brush strokes.

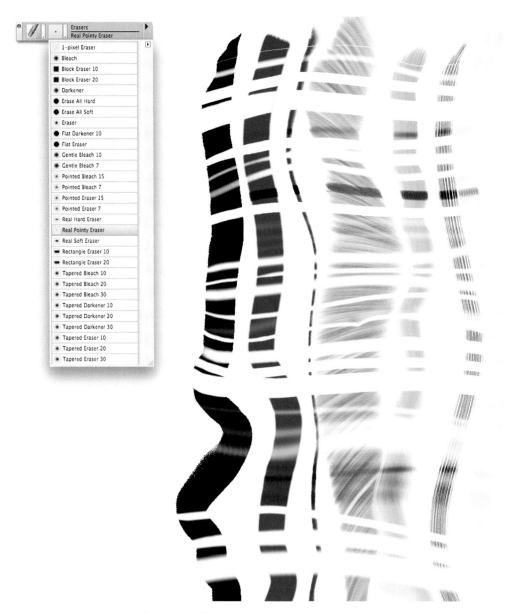

Figure 2.16 *Erasers*—I like the subtlety of Bleach and Gentle Bleach, applied with low stylus pressure.

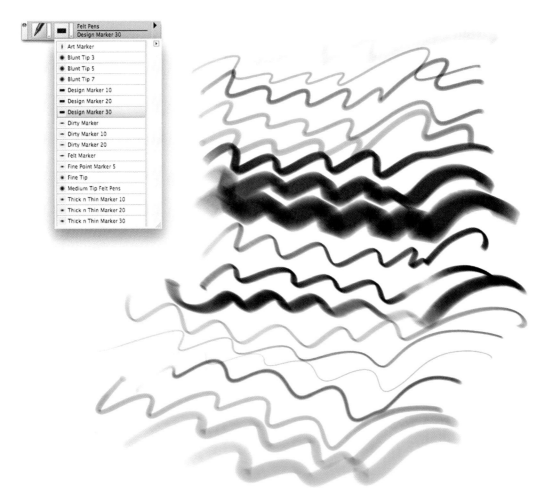

Figure 2.17 *Felt Pens*—Big, fat, fast and bold: that's the Design Marker 30. Builds up to black very rapidly.

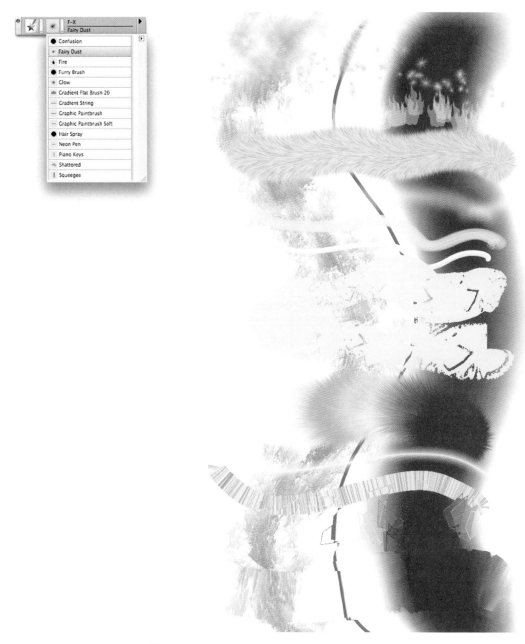

Figure 2.18 *F-X*—Lots of fun brushes, but two that stand out for me are Fairy Dust, perfect for any child-related art, and Glow, a great way to subtly paint in shafts of light.

Figure 2.19 *Gouache*—Want a smooth, quick and hairy brush? Then try the Wet Gouache Round 30.

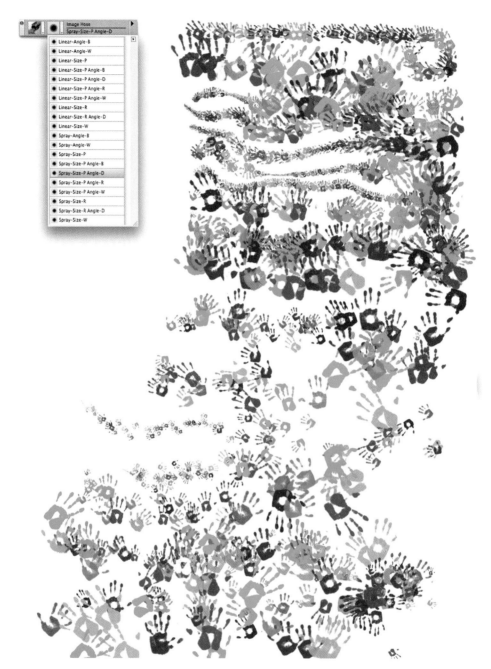

Figure 2.20 *Image Hose*—A wonderful oddity! A brush that spews out image elements from image sets known as "nozzles." The variants control the way the image elements are released onto the canvas. Choose your nozzle from the Nozzle Selector, bottom right icon in the Toolbox. The Hand Prints shown here are from the Jeremy Fave Nozzles1 set.

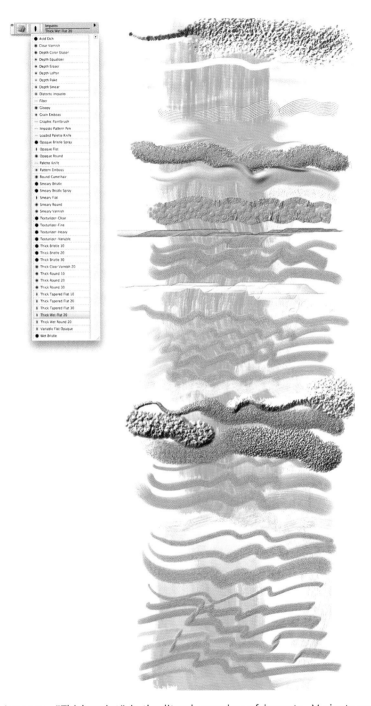

Figure 2.21 *Impasto*—"Thick paint" is the literal meaning of impasto. Variants range from the subtle Wet Bristle, which blends colors as well as adds color, to the characterful Gloopy which fully lives up to its name! The blue star Impasto Toggle Effect button on the upper right of the canvas window frame toggles the Impasto effect, which acts like a mysterious layer, on and off. To preserve impasto and be able to paint over it, save your file as a TIFF file, close it and reopen it.

53

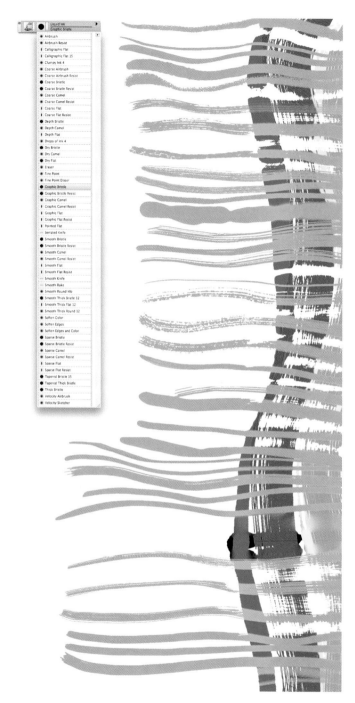

Figure 2.22 *Liquid Ink*—Resolution-independent, bold brush strokes that are editable and etch-able by other Liquid Ink variants, such as resists, while in their special Liquid Ink layer. Graphic Bristle is one of my favorites. Drop the Liquid Ink layer to flatten the image and be able to paint over the Liquid Ink brush strokes with other types of brushes.

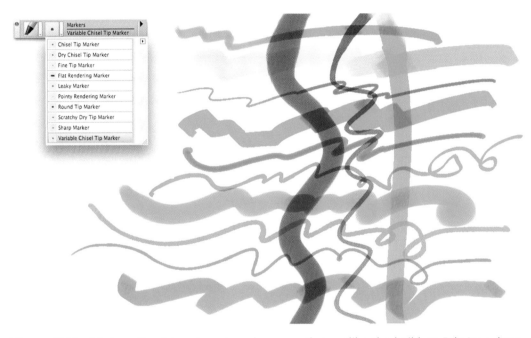

Figure 2.23 *Marker*—Great translucent marker pens that, unlike the build-up Felt Pens, keep their translucent color even as you overlay brush strokes. Good for quickly filling in a line drawing, draft outlines or a sketch.

Figure 2.24 *Oils*—Thick Wet Camel is a great impasto brush that has a thick raised bristle texture within the brush stroke. The Bristle Oils 30 is similar, but smoother, without the impasto effect. Both variants look best when used with the Sample Multiple Colors dropper tool in the Mixer Pad to choose multiple colors across the brush stroke.

Figure 2.25 *Oil Pastels*—The Real Soft Pastel offers an effect similar to the Square Chalk 35 but with the additional Hard Media responsivity to the pen tilt angle.

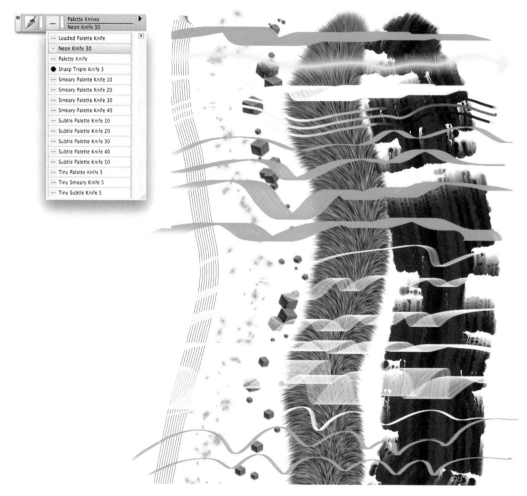

Figure 2.26 *Palette Knives*—My two favorites here are the Sharp Triple Knife 3, great for cross hatching effects, and the Neon Knife 30, which picks up whatever color the stroke starts on.

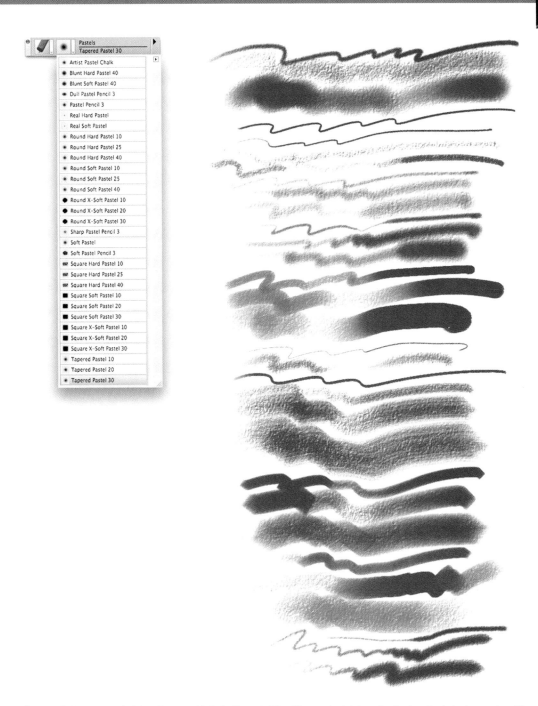

Figure 2.27 *Pastel*—The Square-X Soft Pastel 30 offers a bold brush stroke that fades out with lighter pressure. Square Hard Pastel 40 is great for quick coverage of a large area with paper texture.

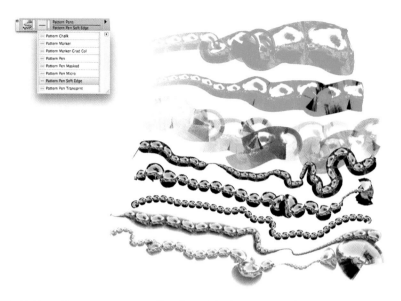

Figure 2.28 *Pattern Pen*—These pens all paint with the current clone source, which, by default, will be the current pattern. Try using the Pattern Pen Soft Edge with one of your paintings set as clone source....

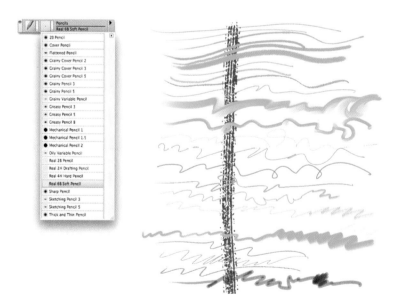

Figure 2.29 *Pencils*—I have two stand out faves in this category: the Real 6B Soft Pencil—just experience the beautiful effect when you tilt your pen; and the Greasy Pencil 5—a smooth oily mark that flows like melted butter.

Figure 2.30 *Pens*—Many variants in this category are similar to the Calligraphy variants. There is still nothing quite like the ultimate smoothness of the Scratchboard tool.

Figure 2.31 *Photo*—The workhorse tools for me in this category are the Dodge, for lightening, and Burn, for darkening. Use them sparingly and lightly. The Saturation Add variant seems to be able to ferret out color in your image where you didn't even think it existed.

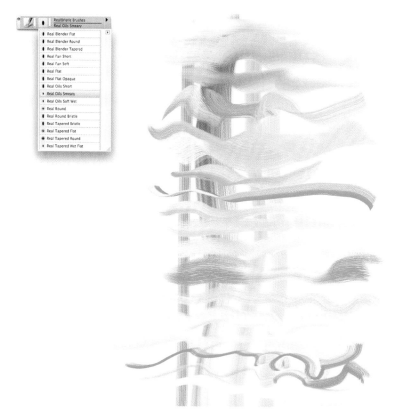

Figure 2.32 *Real Bristle Brushes*—The Real Fan Short and Real Fan Soft both show off the capabilities of the 6D Art Pen and multiple color sampling. Check out the great bristle behavior of many of the variants in this category.

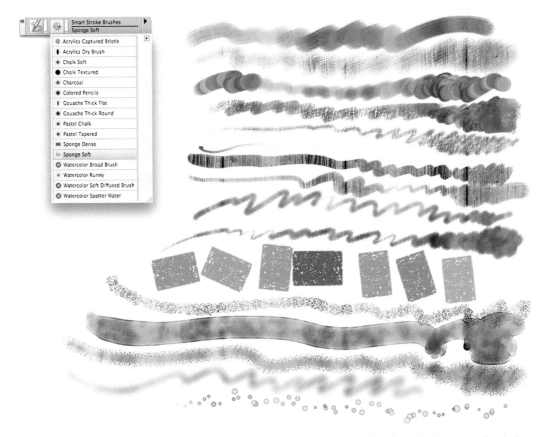

Figure 2.33 *Smart Stroke Brushes*—These brushes are automatically selected when you check the Smart Stroke Painting and Smart Settings checkboxes in the Auto-Painting palette. The Colored Pencil variant brush stroke is like a chameleon, taking on a tint of whatever color it is moving over.

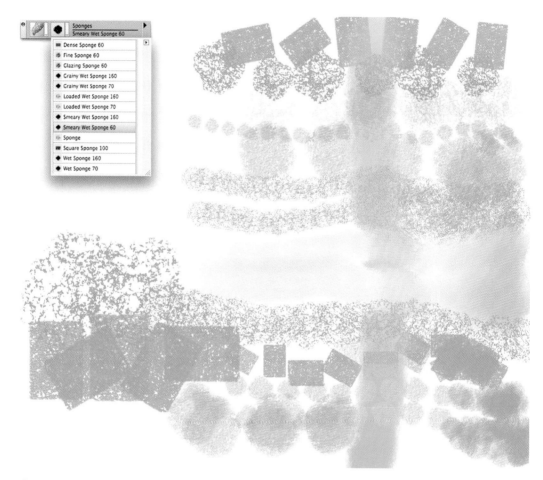

Figure 2.34 *Sponges*—These brushes make me think of SpongeBob turned into a paint brush, especially variants like Square Sponge 100. Smeary Wet Sponge 60 is good for quick mushing up of large areas of canvas.

Figure 2.35 *Sumi-e*—The Coarse Bristle Sumi-e brush variant is probably the closest to an actual sumi-e brush loaded with ink. See how sensitive it is to pressure.

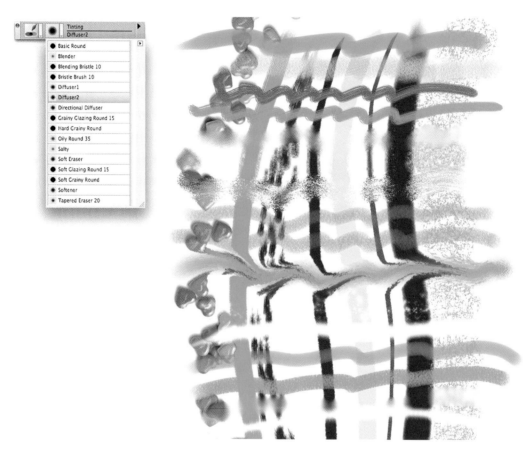

Figure 2.36 *Tinting*—A motley assortment of brushes, my top favorites of which are Diffuser2, a great brush for getting a diffuse watercolor edge look, and Salty which, as the name suggests, is like sprinkling salt crystals on your paint and seeing the crystals absorb the pigment, creating bleached out spots.

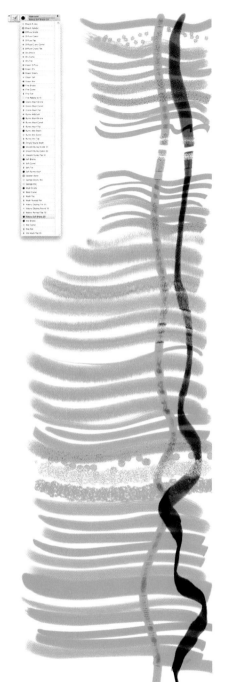

Figure 2.37 *Watercolor*—What a lot of variants in this category: over 50! A couple of the unique looks only found in this category include the Splatter Water and Diffuse Camel. Like the Liquid Inks, these brushes are in a special layer that shows up in the Layers palette. Also like the Liquid Inks, when you wish to paint over your Watercolor brush marks with other types of brushes one of the simplest ways is to drop (flatten) the Watercolor layer.

Figure 2.38 *JeremyFaves2*—This is the category contained in the Resource Disc that comes with this book. As the name suggests, all the brushes it contains are favorites of mine! Stand outs include my students' all-time favorite "Den Laurent's Oil Funky Chunky"—good for oil painting with rich texture; Sherron Shephard's "Blender Wood" for initially covering large areas of the canvas in a loose, gestural way; "Modern Art in a Can," which is better experienced than described, and my own "Jeremy's SumiPollock Splash."

Figure 2.39 *JeremyBoxSet1*—This is the brush set I created specially for PaintboxJ members. Favorites include "Jeremy'sMangaBirdNest" and "JeremyStarSplatter."

Figure 2.40 *JeremyGuestFaves4*—From my *How to Paint from Photographs Using Corel Painter X* DVD, includes David Gell's great "Sui Riu," Greg Gyulai's "geometric web" and the cool "Splatter Smooth."

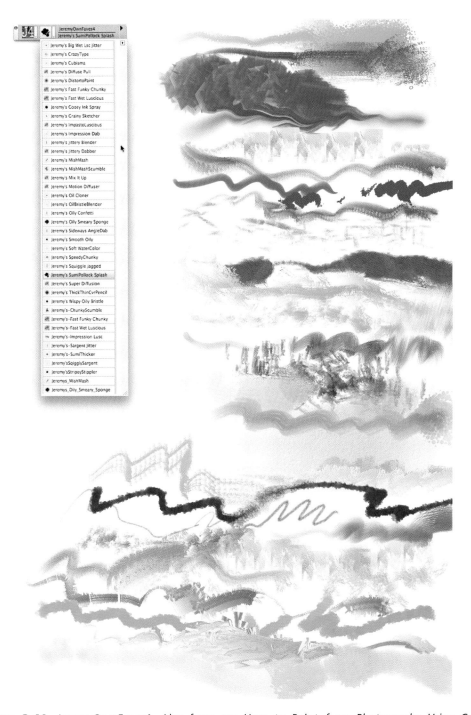

Figure 2.41 *JeremyOwnFaves4*—Also from my *How to Paint from Photographs Using Corel Painter X* DVD, includes brushes not found elsewhere, such as "Jeremy's Jittery Dabber," which is like an explosive oily dabber on steroids!

3

Dive In

Get to Know the Brushes

Now it's time to have some fun! Having whet your appetite with the visual overview of the Brush Guide, we're going to start off with something very simple: exploring the incredible diversity of marks you can make using the myriad of brush variants available at your fingertips.

If you're beginning from scratch, open a new canvas:

1 Choose File > New or keyboard shortcut Cmd-N (Mac)/Ctrl-N (PC).

2 In the New Image dialog window set the width and height units to inches.

3 Set the Width to 16 inches and the height to 11 inches (Figure 3.1).

4 Set the Resolution to 200 pixels per inch.

5 Leave Paper Color white and Picture Type: Image.

6 Click OK.

7 Choose Window > Screen Mode Toggle or use the keyboard shortcut Cmd-M (Mac)/Ctrl-M (PC). This command is near the bottom of the Window menu. It will mount your canvas on your screen.

If you've still got your 16 × 11 canvas open in Painter from Chapter 1, start here:

8 Choose File > Save As or keyboard shortcut Cmd-Shift-S (Mac)/Ctrl-Shift-S (PC).

9 In the Save As dialog window browse to the location where you would like to set up a folder for all your Painter 11 Creativity projects. If in doubt, choose the Desktop.

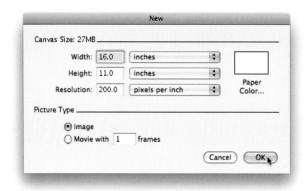

Figure 3.1 New canvas window.

10 Click on the New Folder button (Mac)/icon (PC) in the Save As dialog window.

11 Name your folder "P11C_Projects."

12 Within this folder create your first project folder, titled "YY-MM_BrushExploration," where YY is the year and MM is the month you begin the project (for instance, the title, if you start in May, 2010, will be "10-05_BrushExploration").

13 Name this first version of your image, even if it is just a blank canvas, "explr-01-blank" (Figure 3.2). The last part of this name, "blank," could be replaced, for instance, by an abbreviated note of what category and variant you have currently selected. This name structure follows my P-V-N file naming system, where:

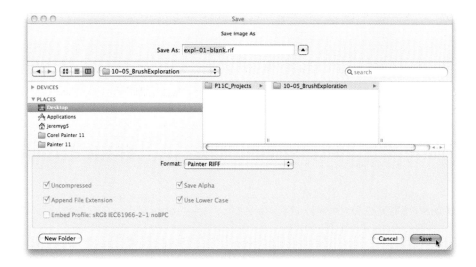

Figure 3.2 The Save As window.

P: compact Project name, preferably five characters or less

V: sequential Version number starting at 01

N: short abbreviated Note about what you just did, used, applied; size and resolution, etc.

Regularly use Save As

As you work on any project, continue to regularly use Save As (*not* Save) and consistently name each saved version with the P-V-N naming system. The reason that I encourage you to use Save As with the P-V-N system, rather than Save, is to document and preserve your creative process. This will empower you down the road, allowing you much greater free-dom in mixing different stages of your painting.

14 Choose the file format Painter RIFF. This is the safest format generally for any work in Painter. RIFFs are the native format of Painter and preserve the editability in reopened files of every special Painter layer and canvas property, including Watercolor, Liquid Ink, Digital Watercolor, Impasto, Text and Mosaics. RIFFs cannot be opened in many other applications and therefore you will always want to back up your final versions in another format such as TIFF or PSD (Photoshop).

15 Click Save.

16 Choose Window > Screen Mode Toggle or use the keyboard shortcut Cmd-M (Mac)/Ctrl-M (PC). This command is near the bottom of the Window menu. It will mount your canvas on your screen.

Create an Abstract

Create an abstract by trying out different brush variants from different categories, using any colors you wish. Try out the different ways of picking color (outlined below). See which brushes work with the Mixer's Sample Multiple Colors tool. For each variant you use, vary the way you apply your brush strokes—soft versus hard, slow versus fast, small brush size versus large, and short dabs versus long strokes. Experiment with the sliders in the Property Bar palette (along the top of your Painter desktop) and see how changing the slider values affects the quality of your marks. Be fearless and push the limits of each brush. You won't break the brush or your tablet. The worst that can happen is that you make a memory intensive brush very large and have to wait a while for it to complete a brush stroke.

How to Restore a Variant to Default Settings

Anytime you wish to restore the default settings for the current variant, just click on the Reset Tool icon in the far left of the Property Bar. The Reset Tool icon looks identical to the Brush icon in the top left corner of the Toolbox. Clicking on the Reset Tool icon is equivalent to choosing Restore Default Variant from the Brush Selector palette pop-up menu.

Fill the Canvas

Don't Undo! Fill your canvas with brush strokes, building up brush strokes on brush strokes. When you come across brushes that don't behave as you expect, or you get the Liquid Ink or Watercolor layer error message, refer back to the Brush Guide (Chapter 2).

Familiarize Yourself with Different Ways to Pick Color

After you are comfortable playing with the brush properties and experimenting with different variants, try out different ways of choosing and influencing color. Practice using the Dropper tool and the Colors, Mixer, Color Sets and Color Variability palettes. Continue building on your "BrushExploration" canvas without undoing and continue to save sequential versions, using Save As, every five or ten minutes.

Main Color versus Clone Color

As you experiment with different ways to pick color, keep exploring and trying out brush variants. You will find that not all brushes paint with the currently selected main color. There are brushes that don't paint color at all but instead move, smear, alter or distort color already on the canvas. There are other brushes, such as the Cloners and Pattern Pens (Figure 3.3), that by default paint with clone color, not the Main Color in the Colors palette. Clone color is color that comes from a clone source. To find out what the clone source is go to File > Clone Source and there will be a check mark by the current clone source. The default clone source in Painter is the current pattern (which you can see previewed in the Window > Library Palettes > Patterns palette).

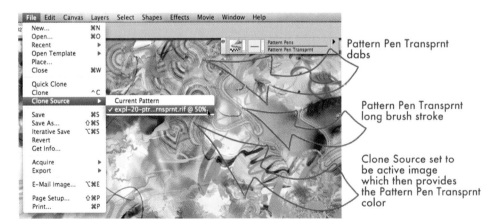

Figure 3.3 The Pattern Pens are examples of brushes that paint with the current clone source, not the Main Color. You can see in this example what happens if you make your active image the clone source as you paint with a Pattern Pen. Note the dramatic difference between the effect of making a short dab brush stroke versus a long brush stroke.

The default pattern is an image of a gray-green succulent plant known as "Hens and Chicks." If you find yourself inadvertently painting with that pattern you now know why!

The variants in the Cloners category are set with Clone Color as the default. You can toggle between Main Color and Clone Color for any brush that paints color by clicking on the Clone Color icon (which looks like the Photoshop Rubber Stamp tool) in the lower right of the Colors palette, or clicking the "U" key. When the Clone Color icon is active, the Hue Ring, Saturation/Value Triangle and Main and Additional color squares in the Colors palette are grayed out, which is usually a sign you are using a brush with Clone Color. The exceptions are the Soft Cloner and Straight Cloner in the Cloners category, which show a fully saturated Colors palette even though they paint using Clone Color. We will be looking at cloners in more detail in subsequent chapters.

Dropper Tool

In the Toolbox, click on the Dropper tool, situated near the bottom of the tools, just above the Magnifier. With the Dropper tool selected in the Toolbox, click in your canvas at a point which has a color you wish to pick. That color will then become the main color, which you can see in the Main Color square of the Colors palette. The small innocuous Dropper is an immensely powerful tool for painting. I use this repeatedly in my painting process to pick local color from within my painting.

There are two keyboard shortcuts you can use to select the Dropper tool. The safest one is the "D" key on your keyboard. Clicking on the "D" automatically selects the Dropper tool in your Toolbox. To return to the brush after you've picked the color you want just click on the "B" key, which is the shortcut for the Brush tool.

The second keyboard shortcut is one that temporarily turns the brush cursor into the Dropper tool while you hold down the Option (Mac)/Alt (PC) key. This shortcut only works once you have paused from painting and lifted your pen tip slightly from the tablet, and provided you are not using Clone Color.

Colors Palette

Color can be defined in a number of ways, such as by combinations of three primary colors (which are red, green and blue when viewing an image within Painter) or by combinations of hue (the named color), saturation (the purity or intensity of color) and value (the lightness or darkness of color). The Colors palette is set up to allow you to easily choose the hue (moving the cursor on the Hue Ring), the saturation (varying the second cursor horizontally across the Saturation/Value Triangle) and the value (varying the second cursor vertically up and down the Saturation/Value Triangle).

If your Saturation/Value Triangle cursor is in either the top left corner (pure white) or bottom left corner (pure black) then it doesn't make any difference what hue you pick. The combination of Hue Ring and Saturation/Value Triangle offers an intuitive way to pick color with a built-in color wheel that is handy for applying color schemes such as juxtaposing complementary colors (colors from opposite sides of the color wheel that add vibrancy to a painting when placed next to each other). A nice new feature introduced in Corel Painter 11 is the ability to expand the Colors palette. Just drag the Color palette by its title bar out of the group of color palettes. Once it is unattached to any other palettes you can then expand it by dragging down and to the right from the bottom right corner. Expanding the Colors palette allows you to have very fine control of the Saturation/Value cursor (which you can also nudge with the arrow keys).

The tricky part of the Colors palette is the two overlapping Additional and Main Color squares. Though they resemble the Background and Foreground color swatches in Adobe Photoshop, their functions are quite different. Most brushes that paint color (as opposed to those that blend, move or distort color already on the canvas) will paint with the currently selected Main Color unless they are cloning and are using a clone source as a means of determining color. The Cloners category of brushes are preset to use Clone Color. Any brush can be turned into a cloner brush by clicking on the Clone Color icon (the one that looks like a rubber stamp), or by using the keyboard shortcut "u." When the Clone Color icon is active the Hue Ring and Saturation/Value Triangle are inactive and usually grayed out.

I recommend that you always make sure the Main Color, the square that is in front, is the active square. Do this by clicking on the Main Color square. Nothing indicates that it is active except you'll notice that it changes color as you change color in the Hue Ring and the Saturation/Value Triangle. The Additional Color square has a bold black outline when active.

The Additional Color square is useful when you wish to go between two colors, such as black and white when painting into a layer mask, or when using one of the few brushes that use both Additional and Main Color (such as F-X > Gradient Flat Brush 20 and Gradient String, Pens > Grad Pen and Grad Repeat Pen), when applying the Two-Tone Gradient and when painting with the Image Hose brushes with reduced Grain. I generally make use of the Color Swap icon to swap the Main and Additional Colors (or use the keyboard shortcut Shift-X).

Mixer Palette

The Mixer palette offers the closest parallel to the traditional Painter's palette. Using its own separate set of tools, you can paint any colors you wish onto the Mixer Pad, choosing colors from the Mixer Colors, a collection of color swatches across the top of the palette, or from the Colors or Color Sets palettes, or from using the Toolbox palette Dropper tool in the active image. You can use the Mixer Palette Knife tool to mix and blend colors in the Mixer Pad and then use the Mixer palette Sample Color dropper tool to select the Main Color from the Mixer Pad. One of the most astounding features of this Mixer palette is when you use the Mixer palette's Sample Multiple Colors dropper tool (Figure 3.4) in combination with certain brushes. For instance:

1 Choose the Gouache > Fine Bristle 30. Choose the Sample Multiple Colors dropper tool (the icon looks like a Dropper tool with a circle at the bottom).

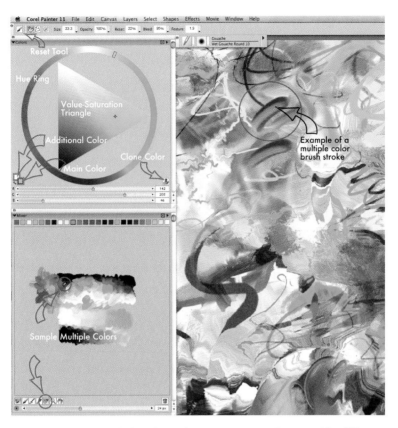

Figure 3.4 Fill your canvas with brush strokes as you experiment with different variants and ways to pick color. This example shows the use of the Sample Multiple Colors Mixer tool being used with the Gouache > Wet Gouache Round 10 variant.

2 Set the Mixer Palette Brush Size slider to the right. This increases the area in the Mixer Pad from which multiple colors will be selected.

3 Click in the Mixer Pad in a region where you wish to select multiple colors.

4 Now paint on your canvas and you will see how multiple colors are distributed across the brush stroke, just as you would expect if a brush were loaded with multiple colors.

The Sample Multiple Colors dropper tool only works with certain brushes. It does not affect the Main Color. Brushes that work with the Multiple Colors dropper tool include:

- Acrylics > Thick Acrylic Bristles, Flats and Rounds;
- Art Pen Brushes > Soft Flat Oils, Tapered Camel and Gouache;
- Artists' Oils > almost all;
- Gouache > Detail and Flat Opaques, Fine Bristles and Rounds, Thick and Wet Gouaches;
- Impasto > Opaque Bristle Spray, Opaque Flat and Opaque Round, and all the Smeary brushes;

- Oils > Bristle Oils, Fine Camel, Flat Oil, Glazing Flat, Round Camel Hair, Smearys and Thick Oils;
- RealBristle Brushes > almost all except blenders;
- Smart Stroke Brushes > Gouaches when not cloning.

Note that the Sample Color and Sample Multiple Colors dropper tools in the Mixer palette are distinct from the Dropper tool in the Toolbox. The Mixer droppers only sample from the Mixer Pad, not from your main image.

Just as with the Colors palette, you can also expand the Mixer palette in Painter 11. Drag the Mixer palette by its title bar out from the group of color palettes, and then expand it by dragging down and to the right from the bottom right corner. Notice how the number of Mixer Color swatches across the top of the palette increases as you expand the palette.

Once you have created a mix of colors you like in the Mixer Pad you can save the Mixer Pad by choosing Save Mixer Pad in the Mixer pop-up menu. You clear your Mixer Pad by choosing Clear Mixer Pad from the same menu.

Color Sets Palette

Color sets allow you to conveniently access a particular range of colors and easily pick those colors just by clicking on the color squares. They are ideal for keeping consistency of colors throughout a project or expanding your use of colors to include those you may not otherwise choose. They can also help you challenge yourself by limiting your range of colors.

They are intuitive and simple to use since you see a small swatch of the color you are picking and you don't need to mix or create the colors. There are many different extra color sets supplied with Painter and on the Resource Disc at the back of this book. It is easy to create your own custom color sets from existing imagery or the Mixer Pad.

The factory default color set is the Artists' Oils Colors which you will find in the Corel Painter 11 > Support Files > Color Sets. It is based on traditional oil paint colors. You can toggle the display of the color names on and off by opening the Color Sets pop-up menu (click on small solid black triangle in upper right of palette) and choosing Display Names. From the same Color Sets pop-up menu you can also customize the color swatch size by choosing Swatch Size > Customize and adjusting the swatch height and width for optimum viewing.

To access other color sets:

1 Choose Open Color Set from the pop-up menu.
2 You will see an ominous-sounding message that says "Loading a new Color Set will overwrite your current Painter Colors.colors, and any changes you have made will be lost." Provided you haven't made any customizations to the current color set, just go ahead and choose Load. If you have made changes that you want to keep, choose Cancel and, from the Color Set pop-up menu, Save Color Set.

3 Choose the application folder Corel Painter 11 > Support Files > Color Sets, where you'll find the default Artists' Oils Colors color set (Figure 3.5) should you wish to return to it later and Jeremy Color Sets2 (where you'll find some color sets I have made from historic master paintings).

Figure 3.5 Choosing and controlling color sets.

4 Select a color set from those listed within the folder.

5 Choose Open. The selected color set now appears in the Color Sets palette.

You can edit any color set, adding or taking away colors, at any time from within the Color Sets palette. Adding colors to a color set as you work can be useful in building up a color set of your favorite colors over time.

It can be valuable to emulate, or limit yourself to, the color palette of an artist. Color sets make it easy to do this.

1 Open an image whose colors you wish to capture in a custom color set.

2 Select New Color Set from Image from the lower left-hand icon pop-up menu in the Color Sets palette. This will automatically generate a custom color set based on the colors in the current active image.

3 Choose Save Color Set from the same pop-up menu.

You can also generate a color set from your current Mixer Pad by choosing New Color Set from Mixer Pad. After creating a custom color set choose Save Color Set, give it a suitable name, and save it in the Color Sets folder (or any other location).

Color Variability Palette

This small but powerful palette includes three sliders that either add variation of hue, saturation and value within a brush stroke as it progresses, as in the case of the Pencils > Real 6B Soft Pencil, or add variation of those color parameters in successive brush strokes, as in the case of Oils > Medium Bristle Oils 15 (Figure 3.6).

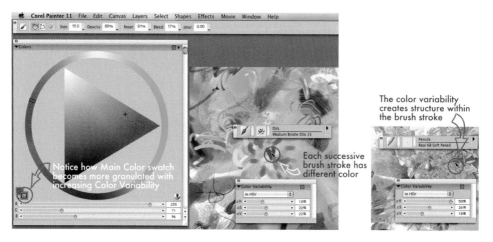

Figure 3.6 Two contrasting examples of how Color Variability affects brush stroke color.

Experiment with the Brush Controls

The properties that appear in the Property Bar for each brush variant are a small subset of the vast array of customizable settings contained in the Brush Controls palettes (Window > Brush Controls > ...). The Brush Controls contain all the settings that determine the behavior of each variant in Painter. They can be a little intimidating at first sight but are fascinating to explore. In my workspace arrangement, you'll find the Brush Controls palettes beneath the Size palette (which is one of the Brush Controls). Minimize the Size palette (click on arrow in top left) or drag down the bottom right corner of the Size palette window to view the full set of Brush Controls palettes.

Choose a brush variant you like and start experimenting with the Brush Controls, testing their effect. You'll find that not all controls are applicable to all brushes and they will be grayed out when not applicable.

Keep building up brush marks on your "BrushExploration" canvas as you experiment with the Brush Controls in this exercise. Every 10 minutes or so, choose Save As and save the current state of your canvas, maintaining the consistent P-V-N file naming system with sequential version numbers (01, 02, and so on).

One further level of brush experimentation that you may venture into is the Brush Creator (Cmd-B / Ctrl-B or Window > Show Brush Creator). Look up the article *Getting Started with the Brush Creator* in the Help > Corel Painter 11 Help (Cmd-?/Ctrl-?) for a detailed explanation of how to use the Brush Creator.

Practice Saving Your Own Custom Variants

As you experiment with the sliders in the Property Bar and delve into the Brush Controls palettes, you will find you create custom variants you wish to save for future use. If you don't save a custom variant right away, the chances are you will continue altering the properties of the brush and never be able to recall the exact settings that gave you the effect you liked. Therefore, when you come a across a custom variation you like, follow these instructions to save and organize the custom variant. Practice with at least one custom variant so you can get used to the process.

Save Variant

1 Select Save Variant from the Brush Selector pop-up menu (Figure 3.7).

2 Name the new variant something appropriately descriptive with 23 characters or less (with more than 23 characters the OK button will be grayed out). Adopt an organized custom variant naming system. I recommend you begin each new custom variant name with your initials or first name, so you can easily identify and differentiate your custom variants from the default variants. Choose variant names that convey some sense of the look and feel of the brush.

3 Click OK. The new variant appears, positioned alphabetically, in the current variant list (Figure 3.7). It can be conveniently accessed at any time in the future.

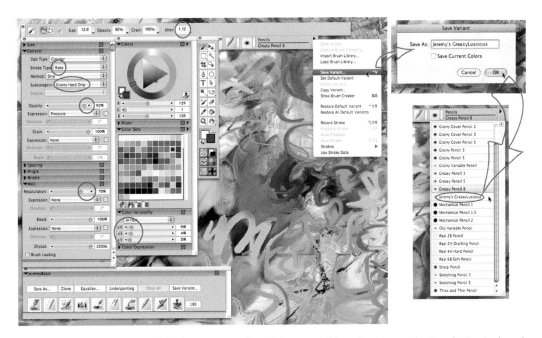

Figure 3.7 Experiment with the Property Bar sliders and, if you're brave, the Brush Controls palettes, and then save your custom variant. The custom settings are highlighted in this example.

Copying a Variant From One Category to Another

1 If you wish to move any variant (custom or default) from one category to another (for instance to group your favorite variants together in one category) then first choose the variant you wish to move. Note that new custom variants are not automatically selected when they are saved.

2 Choose Copy Variant from the Brush Selector pop-up menu.

3 Choose the category into which you wish to copy the variant from the "Copy variant to:" pop-up menu in the Copy Variant window.

4 Click OK.

5 If you now wish to delete the copied variant from the original category (it'll still be the active variant) choose Delete Variant from the Brush Selector pop-up menu. Be careful you don't accidentally delete default variants.

6 If you wish to return any variant to its original factory default settings, select that variant in the Brush Selector.

7 Click on the Reset tool, which looks like a brush icon and is located on the far left of the Property Bar. This resets the current variant to its factory default settings.

Exporting and Backing Up a Custom Variant

To export your custom variants you need to know where the custom files are stored in your computer and which files to copy. This is also important information for backing up your custom data.

1 Before searching on your computer hard drive for your custom data, first, within Painter, look under Window > Workspace and note which workspace is checked. If you haven't imported a workspace, the current workspace may be the one named "Default." Your current workspace includes not only your current palette layout but also every library, custom palette, custom brush variant, preference setting and so on. Knowing the name of your current workspace will allow you to find where the custom variant data are stored.

2 The next step on a Mac is to open the Finder browser window. Open your user folder (user name) > Library > Application Support > Corel > Painter 11 > (current workspace name) > Brushes > Painter Brushes > (category containing the custom variant). PC users choose in the My Computer window Local Disk (C:) > Documents and Settings > user directory (user name) > Application Data > Corel > Painter 11 > (current workspace name) > Brushes > Painter Brushes > (category containing the custom variant). This is where all the custom data associated with any custom variant are saved.

3 Hold down the Cmd/Ctrl key while you select all the files with the custom variant name contained within the folder identified in step 2 above. You may find files ending in .xml, .nib,

.stk and .jpg. Watch out because the .xml file may be listed lower in the folder contents list than the other files and it is easy to accidentally overlook selecting the .xml file.

4 Copy these selected files onto a portable device (such as a thumb drive). Take your portable device to your other computer (or share the files over the web, or email or however you wish to transport them between computers).

5 On the other computer copy these .nib, .stk and .xml files into, for Mac users, Applications > Corel Painter 11 > Brushes > Painter Brushes > category folder, or for PC users: Local Disk (C:) > Programs > Corel > Corel Painter 11 > Brushes > Painter Brushes > category folder. The category folder corresponds to the category you wish to see the custom variant appear in. It will appear at the bottom of the variant list in that category.

Before moving on to the next exercise, choose Save As, add the next version number, and after the version number add the note "abstractFINAL," for example: "explr-27-abstractFINAL.rif" (Figure 3.8).

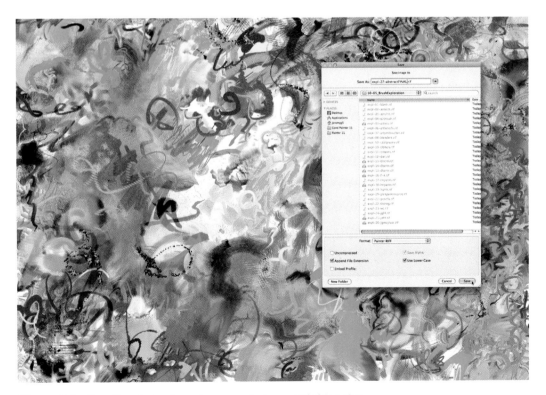

Figure 3.8 Save the abstract you have created up until this point.

Transform the Abstract into a Still Life

1 Position a vase of colorful cut flowers next to your computer screen.

2 Looking back and forth between the flowers and your screen, and without undoing or erasing anything, paint the flowers on top of your abstract (Figure 3.9). See if you can incorporate parts of the abstract. Try using some Distortion brushes to move paint around as well as brushes that simply cover up what is there. Have fun with this! The goal here is not to create a masterpiece or even a close likeness, but simply to express yourself on the canvas, basing your brush marks on what you see.

Figure 3.9 Paint the flowers over the abstract.

3 Remember to use Save As regularly as you build up the still life. Spend at least 30 minutes on this exercise.

4 When you feel you have reached a point of completion choose Save As, add the next version number, and after the version number add the note "flowersFINAL," for example: "explr-36-flowersFINAL.rif."

Transform the Still Life into a Self-Portrait

1 Position a small mirror next to your computer screen angled so that you can see yourself.

2 Looking back and forth between the mirror and your screen, and without undoing or erasing anything, paint a self-portrait on top of your flower still life painting (Figure 3.10). Try using the full area of your canvas and paint to the edges, rather than making a small portrait in the

Figure 3.10   Paint a self-portrait over the flowers.

center. Focus on looking at, and depicting, the shapes of color and value (lights and darks) you see.

3   Remember to Save As regularly as you build up the self-portrait. Spend at least 30 minutes on this exercise.

4   When you feel you have reached a point of completion choose Save As, add the next version number, and after the version number add the note "selfpFINAL," for example: "explr-45-selfpFINAL.rif".

Treat Your Canvas as a Continuously Transforming Surface

In going from abstract to still life to self-portrait, all within one single creative process, you have experienced first hand the power of treating your canvas as a continuously transforming surface in which you can go from any starting point to any ending point. This is empowering since it frees you up on the digital canvas, knowing that nothing is that critical since you can always transform it. I treat my painting process almost as more sculptural than painting, treating the canvas like malleable wet clay that I can keep changing and transforming. I encourage you to adopt this attitude, or at least try it out for a while and see how it works for you.

There is a paradox here. Treating your process as one of continuous transformation and knowing that an image can rise like a phoenix from any abstract mess, does not mean that you don't need to carefully observe your subject or make intentional marks. Once you are focused on depicting a particular subject, whether from direct observation of life, as in the still and self-portrait, or from a reference photograph, then careful observation, intentional brush strokes and continual analysis of what is working or not, and what needs adjusting in your painting, are critical.

To illustrate the continuously transforming nature of my painting process, I share with you here (Figure 3.11) the journey that my canvas went through in following the exercises in this chapter.

Figure 3.11 An overview of the transformations of my canvas.

Have Fun with the Kaleidoscope

1 With your self-portrait painting open in Painter, click on the second icon from the left on the row of icons at the bottom of the Layers palette. This icon, which looks like an electric plug, is the Dynamic Plugins icon. A menu will pop up.

2 Choose Kaleidoscope from the Dynamic Plugins pop-up menu (or Layers > Dynamic Plugins > Kaleidoscope). This generates a special Kaleidoscope Dynamic Plugin layer (signified by a plug layer icon) and automatically changes the current tool from the Brush tool to the Layer Adjuster tool.

3 In the Kaleidoscope window set the size to be 500 by 500 pixels.

4 Move the kaleidoscope square around over your abstract by clicking and dragging with the Layer Adjuster tool.

5 When you find a pattern you like, choose Drop and Select from the Layers pop-up menu (Figure 3.12).

6 Choose Cmd-C/Ctrl-C (Edit > Copy).

7 Choose Edit > Paste into New Image. This makes the kaleidoscope pattern a new image.

8 Save the kaleidoscope pattern image. You could use this as a stand alone artwork or capture it as a pattern and apply it as a repeating tile.

9 Return to the canvas where you generated the kaleidoscope pattern.

10 Choose Cmd-Z/Ctrl-Z (Edit > Undo). This reverses the Drop and Select command and returns the Kaleidoscope to being a separate Dynamic Plugin layer.

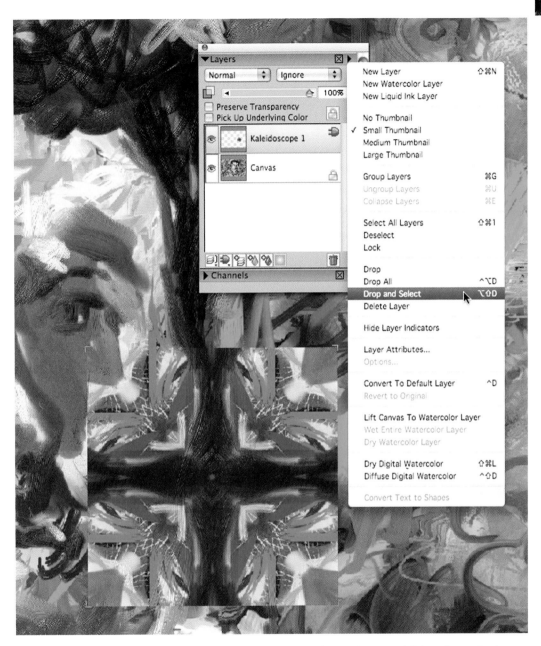

Figure 3.12 When you like the Kaleidoscope pattern, choose Drop and Select from the Layers pop-up menu.

11 You can now continue generating more kaleidoscope patterns or click on the trash can icon in the bottom right of the Layers palette while the Kaleidoscope layer is selected. This will delete the kaleidoscope layer.

Painting From Photos—Preparation

Photography and Painting

Photography has been used by artists since its inception, allowing the capture of transient scenes that may be difficult to capture through sketching or painting alone. The painter can then, using the photograph as reference, take the image to another level with their unique interpretation and style, adding multiple points of view and variations within the painting, and making use of the deep range of colors, tones, details, textures and contrasts offered by paint.

The advent of digital photography and digital painting offers a powerful and exciting combination and virtually unlimited possibilities, some of which we will explore in this and the following few chapters. My goal in this, and the subsequent "Painting from Photos" chapters, is to share my general approach, give you an overview of my workflow and describe the techniques I use in painting from reference photographs, explained with examples of specific projects. I am not intending to give you a fixed recipe to replicate. I suggest you try out the techniques I share and mix them in to your own workflow as and when they are appropriate. Every picture you work on will suggest its own path so be open to "listening and responding" to your painting as it develops and to trying out different techniques, ideas and workflows with different projects.

Figure 4.1 *Waterfall*, painting of a misty waterfall scene in GuangZhou, China.

Figure 4.2 *Generations*, a painting of singer Kim Nalley (on the left) being joined on stage by her Grandmother to sing *When the Saints Go Marching In*.

Imagine and Compose Before You Capture

Your painting process begins before you click the shutter of your camera. Look at the world from the point of view of a painter. Look for interesting shapes, textures, juxtapositions and compositions. Look at the way light falls, is reflected and casts shadows. Look for mood and atmosphere. Imagine the potential paintings as you view the world around you.

When looking at your camera's LCD display preview window, or through the viewfinder, play with framing and composition. Hold your camera horizontally and then vertically and compare the compositions. Zoom in and out and decide what amount of space around your main subject works best. Look at the positive and negative shapes defined by your subject's contours and the edge of your frame. Seek shapes that make interesting abstract forms.

At the moment you see the composition fall into place in your camera preview window or viewfinder, click the shutter (Figure 4.3).

For maximum versatility I recommend taking your photographs in RAW rather than JPG file format, if your camera allows. RAW will give you much more leeway for adjustments than JPG. I also recommend, when possible, setting your camera Color Space to Adobe RGB instead of sRGB.

Choose Your Source Photo

Select a source image that calls out to you to be painted—which moves you and motivates you. For this exercise create a painting for yourself, not for a client, relative or friend. Do not worry about what someone else thinks and whether they'll like what you've created.

If you are choosing a portrait image, seek out a view that captures an emotion. If you have more than one subject look for compositions which relate to each other, rather than just with the camera. If you are choosing from a large number of potential photographs it is handy to use some form of a browsing program such as Apple Aperture, Adobe Lightroom, Adobe Bridge, and Microsoft Expression Media.

If using RAW files, open your chosen source photograph in Adobe Camera Raw, or an equivalent Raw browser.

1 If in Adobe Camera Raw (Figure 4.6), click with the White Balance tool (third icon from the left on the top row of icons) in a white or gray area of the image. See the effect and adjust the Color Temperature slider as needed.
2 Adjust the Exposure and Fill Light sliders to see if they improve the image and allow more detail to be seen.
3 Open the resulting image in Adobe Photoshop. If you do not have Photoshop open your source photograph in Painter.
4 Choose File > Save As, or use keyboard shortcut Shift-Cmd-S (Mac)/Shift-Ctrl-S (PC).

Figure 4.3 The original photograph upon which *Waterfall* was based. The scene was cropped in the camera's frame to provide a composition that comprised three main regions: foreground lake, mid-ground cliff face with foliage and waterfall, and the background sky. The bridge and the walkway divide the vertical space of the composition by the Golden Section, also known as the "Divine Proportion."

5 Save this source file as a flat RGB TIFF file with the P-V-N file naming convention (ProjectName-01-srcimg.tif) in a new project folder called "YY-MM ProjectName," within the "P11C_Projects" folder, where YY is the year, MM is the month and ProjectName is whatever project name is appropriate for your image subject.

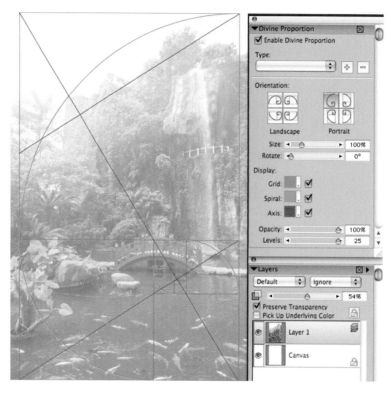

Figure 4.4 Using Window > Divine Proportion to access the Divine Proportion palette, and with Enable Divine Proportion checked (which makes the Divine Proportion overlay visible), you can see the how the bridge divides the composition vertically by the Divine Proportion ratio. To allow you to see the Divine Proportion overlay more clearly, I chose Select > All, Select > Float and then lowered the layer opacity.

Enhance Contrast and Saturation (Photoshop)

1 In Photoshop choose Layer > New Adjustment Layer > Levels.

2 Adjust the Levels' black and white points to increase contrast.

3 Choose Layer > New Adjustment Layer > Hue/Saturation.

4 Increase the Saturation slider slightly.

5 Choose File > Save As, or use keyboard shortcut Shift-Cmd-S (Mac)/Shift-Ctrl-S (PC).

6 Save the layered RGB Photoshop file with name "ProjectName-02-adjlyrs.psd" in the new project folder.

7 Choose Flatten from the Layer menu.

8 Choose File > Save As, or use keyboard shortcut Shift-Cmd-S (Mac)/Shift-Ctrl-S (PC).

9 Save as a flat RGB TIFF file with name "ProjectName-03-srcimgflat.tif."

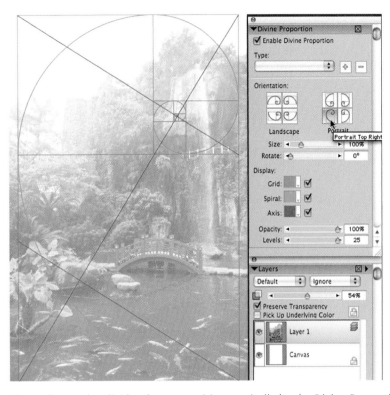

Figure 4.5 The walkway also divides the composition vertically by the Divine Proportion ratio.

Tune into Your Source Photo

1 Mount your selected source image on your screen (in Photoshop: click the F key repeatedly until your photo is mounted against black; in Painter: choose Cmd-M/Ctrl-M).

2 Choose Cmd-0/Ctrl-0 (that's the numeral zero "0", not the letter "o") to zoom to fit.

3 Choose the Tab key to hide all palettes, and, if needed, Cmd-R/Ctrl-R to hide rulers.

4 Get out of your chair and step away from your computer. Look back at your screen from a distance. Half close your eyes and see your source image in terms of lights and darks only. Slowly walk back towards your screen. Stop periodically and contemplate your image. Tune into the feeling of the picture and visualize the painting you wish to create. Ask yourself the following questions:

- What emotion and mood does it convey?
- What story does it ask you to tell?
- Where do you want to go with this image?
- What are the main points of interest?

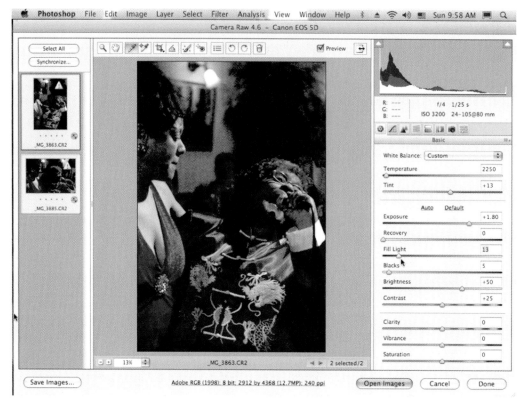

Figure 4.6 The source photos used in *Generations* opened in Adobe Photoshop Camera Raw. The Custom White Balance dropper tool has been used to adjust the color balance. The Exposure has been increased slightly and Fill Light used to bring out mid-tone detail. I liked the emotion and passion captured in the image you see in the Camera Raw preview window, and the way that Kim is relating to her Grandmother. The second photo captures an expression on Kim's face I wanted to use in the final composition.

- What do you want to stand out in your painterly interpretation of this photograph?
- Will cropping or adding canvas give a better composition?

Refine Your Composition

It may be that your original source photograph does not need any compositional modification. This was the case in *Waterfall*. Other times you may find that cropping into the image, or adding extra canvas, can increase the dramatic effect of the composition. Experiment and see what looks best to you. Trust your eye.

You always have the option of cropping your painting once it is complete. I personally prefer to crop before I begin painting, since the way I paint takes into account where the edges are and how the composition intersects with those edges.

To Crop into Your Image

In Photoshop, drag the Crop tool over your image, and adjust the size and proportions of the crop area using the crop control handles prior to pressing the Return (Mac)/Enter (PC) key to make the crop. In Painter, drag the Crop tool in your image and then click inside the crop area to make the crop. You can use the Divine Proportion overlay for additional assistance (Figures 4.4 and 4.5). An alternative in Painter for experimenting with crops is to drag the Rectangular Selection tool over different areas you'd like to crop and in each case choose Edit > Copy followed by Edit > Paste into New Image. This automatically makes your crop a new image.

To Add Extra Canvas to Your Image

In Photoshop, choose Image > Canvas Size, click on the Anchor position to determine which direction you are adding extra canvas to, adjust the width and/or height dimensions, choose your canvas extension color and click OK. In Painter, choose your canvas extension color in the Colors palette, choose Canvas > Set Paper Color, then choose Canvas > Canvas Size, type in the number of pixels you wish added in any direction and click OK.

To Copy and Paste a Section From Another Photo into Your Source Image

In the case of *Generations* I was happy with the overall composition but not with Kim's expression. I wanted to use her expression from a second photo in place of the original expression in my source image. I could have done this in either Photoshop or Painter. I chose to use Painter. I feathered and copied a freehand selection (Figure 4.7) from the second photo and pasted it on the source image. Anything pasted into an image in Painter is automatically pasted in as a layer that appears in the Layers palette. With this layer active I chose Layers > Convert to Reference Layer. I reduced the layer opacity on the Layers palette to about 55% so I could see through the layer to the source image underneath. I used the Layer Adjuster tool to move the layer over the area I wished to replace in the image (Figure 4.8). I held down the Shift key while I adjusted the corner control handles of the Reference layer and resized it to fit exactly over Kim's face underneath.

When I was satisfied with the positioning and size of the Reference layer, and had adjusted the layer opacity back up to 100%, I then dropped the layer, saving the flat image as a TIFF file with the next sequential version number.

Determine Size and Resolution

"What resolution should I work at for painting?" This is a question I am asked frequently and I will do my best to answer it. Any discussion of resolution must start with understanding file size. The "size" of a digital image can mean the following:

1   The **total number of pixels** in the file. Pixels are the basic building blocks of a digital image. Each pixel defines the color specification (such as hue, saturation and value) within a

Figure 4.7 After making a freehand selection around Kim's head I feathered the selection with a 30 pixel feather value.

Figure 4.8 Moving the Reference layer into position over the original photo.

particular tile in an array of tiles that make up the image. The pixel file size is usually measured in units of megapixels. This unit of size is most commonly used in connection with digital camera specifications.

2 How much **computer memory** the file occupies, normally measured in megabytes (MB), or gigabytes (GB). These units of size is most commonly used when storing and transferring image data.

3 Since the pixels in a digital image are arranged in a rectangular array, another way of defining file size is by specifying the **horizontal and vertical dimensions (width and height)**. These two dimensions can be specified either in **pixels** only, or in a combination of **physical length**, such as inches, combined with the **pixel resolution** which defines the number of pixels in each unit of physical length, such as pixels per inch (PPI). Note that the "physical length" specified here is simply a theoretical physical length, and is not manifested until the digital file is printed. These units of width and height in pixels and in physical length and pixel resolution are the units that are of most relevance and concern to us as digital artists.

First Set Your Target Physical Dimensions

Think ahead to what print dimensions you wish to end up with. This will then determine what file dimensions to start with. If you are not sure what final dimensions you want, I suggest aiming at something at least roughly 16 inches by 24 inches. Most of my work ends up being printed between 30 inches by 40 inches up to approximately 40 inches by 60 inches. Since my Epson 9600 printer accepts 44 inches wide canvas rolls and I like to allow at least 3 inches or so of extra canvas around my final image for stretching, I generally keep within a width of 38 inches. My choice of dimensions, besides utilizing my in-house printing technology to the maximum dimensions it can offer me, is also a scale at which I find my paintings work well.

To begin with, set your end goal in physical dimensions (inches) without changing the total number of pixels.

1 In Photoshop choose Image > Image Size, keyboard shortcut Option-Cmd-I (Mac)/Alt-Ctrl-I (PC).
2 Uncheck Resample Image. This ensures you initially do not alter the total number of pixels in the image.
3 Set the units of Width and Height to be Inches if they are not already (you can set this as default in the Preferences > General).
4 Set the Width and Height dimensions to be the final printed dimensions you are aiming for. The Resolution (pixels per inch) will change to keep the total number of pixels constant. In the Image Size dialog window you can now see at the top the number of pixels (width by height) and below, the current physical dimensions and pixel resolution. This gives you all the information you need to make your next choice: whether to resample (equivalent to resize) your image or not and change the total number of pixels.

If you do not have Photoshop the equivalent operation in Painter is:

1 In Painter choose Canvas > Resize or keyboard shortcut Shift-Cmd-R (Mac)/Shift-Ctrl-R (PC).
2 Make sure Constrain File Size is checked.

3 Set the units of Width and Height to be Inches if they are not already (you can set this as default in the Preferences > General).

4 Set the Width and Height dimensions to be the final printed dimensions you are aiming for. The Resolution (pixels per inch) will change to keep the total number of pixels constant. Unfortunately the Painter Resize dialog window, unlike the Photoshop Image Size dialog window, does not show you the pixel width and height and physical dimensions width and height at the same time.

To Resize or Not Resize

When you resize or resample an image, you are changing the total number of pixels in the image. If you resize up you are adding pixels that weren't there previously, and if you are resizing down you are losing pixels that you originally captured in your camera. From the computer's point of view all that counts is the total number of pixels in an image file since this determines the amount of data that the computer needs to process, which in turn affects the response speed of the brushes in Painter, how large the brush size can be made relative to the image size and the quality of the printed artwork. Early in the painting process I like to be able to paint large, loose, fast responding brush strokes and therefore I do not want my file size to be too big. On the other hand, if your file is too small you'll find pixelation when you zoom in, which limits, for instance, the fine detail you can add in the eyes of a portrait. Also, if your file is too small and you later resize to a much larger size you may see softening and degradation of image quality.

In general I like to have at least 2000 pixels along the shortest side of the image (width or height) but no more than about 8000 pixels along the longest side, depending on the power and speed of the computer and the physical size of the final artwork I wish to print. Please note that there can always be exceptions, depending on the final effect you want. Generally I do not reduce the number of pixels I already have from my camera, but will sometimes increase the number. Over the years I have made prints from digital files with a wide variety of pixel resolutions, ranging from as low as 72 PPI (for a large 8 feet by 10 feet Vutek banner print which was designed to be viewed from a distance) up to 360 PPI. Whilst more pixel resolution will generally result in a more detailed print, there is a lot of leeway with digital paintings. As a general guide I suggest aiming at about 150–200 PPI at final size. As you can see in the *Waterfall* example here (Figure 4.9), I do not always keep to that range and will sometimes work at lower resolution, especially if I am aiming at a large final print, doing a live demonstration or working on my laptop.

To change the pixel resolution while keeping the physical dimensions you have set constant, in the Photoshop Image Size window check Resample Image (Figure 4.9) and then change the pixel resolution, or the pixel width and height, accordingly. The equivalent in Painter is to choose Canvas > Resize and make sure the Constrain File Size box is unchecked. You would need to adjust the width and height units to inches and then you can adjust dimensions or pixel resolution independently.

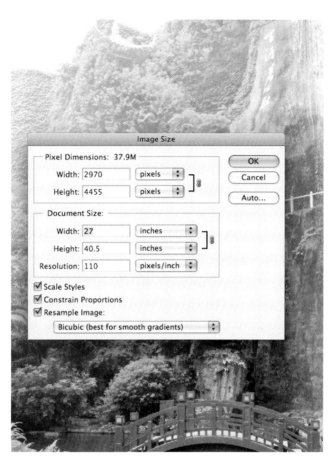

Figure 4.9 The file size of the *Waterfall* source image after resizing up slightly, using the Photoshop Image Size dialog window, from 2912 pixels by 4368 pixels to 27 inches by 40.5 inches at 110 pixels per inch, equivalent to 2970 pixels by 4455 pixels. I kept the overall size relatively low since I was working on this image on my MacBook Pro whilst traveling. The image was not cropped and kept the aspect ratio (4:6) of the original source photograph.

Sometimes my target dimensions are determined by wishing to utilize a standard frame size, or to fit an existing frame I already have. It is not unusual for the dimensions of paintings to be the result of materials that artists happened to have on hand. For instance Dutch artist Rembrandt van Rijn used three standard width horizontal strips of canvas sewn together to make his famous painting *The Night Watch (The Company of Captain Frans Banning Cocq and Lieutenant Willem van Ruytenburch)*, 1642. French painter Édouard Vuillard frequently painted on used cardboard, taken from the bottoms of boxes used by his mother to pack the dresses which she made and sold. Fellow French artists Pierre Bonnard and Toulouse Lautrec also painted on recycled cardboard supports from shirt boxes, and these supports determined the physical dimensions of many of their paintings.

When you wish to fit an exact dimension that has a different aspect ratio (width to height ratio) from your source image, then I recommend using the Crop tool in Photoshop where you can set the dimensions of the crop in inches and the resolution in pixels per inch. Typically most digital cameras provide a digital image with an aspect ratio of 4:6 (or 6:4, depending on portrait

Figure 4.10 The file size of the *Generations* source image after using the Photoshop Crop tool to slightly change the aspect ratio and resize up by almost 50% from a source photo that was 2912 pixels by 4368 pixels to a final cropped source image 30 inches by 40 inches at 150 pixels per inch, equivalent to 4500 pixels by 6000 pixels. In this case I was aiming to use a standard 30 inches by 40 inches frame.

or landscape orientation). In the case of *Generations*, I wanted to fit a 30 inches by 40 inches frame (4.5:6 aspect ratio) so I used the Photoshop Crop tool (see Figure 4.10).

Whatever you end up with once you have made your initial decisions regarding size and pixel resolution, choose Save As and save your file with the next sequential version number followed by a note that summarizes the width, height and resolution, for instance: "ProjectName-04-30×40at150.tif." I find the labeling of the size and resolution in the file name very useful. If you ever resize the image again later in the process, I recommend again labeling the new size and resolution in the file name.

Enhance Contrast and Saturation (Painter)

1 Open the file in Painter.
2 In Painter choose Effects > Tonal Control > Equalize, or use keyboard shortcut Shift-Cmd-E (Mac)/Shift-Ctrl-E (PC) (Figure 4.11).

Figure 4.11 Applying the Equalize effect to the *Waterfall* source photograph in Painter.

3 Click OK. You'll see an automatic enhancement of the contrasts in your image, roughly equivalent to Auto Levels in Photoshop. This Equalize command in Painter is a wonderful tool and I recommend you try it out during your painting process from time to time. You may be surprised at the positive difference it can make.

4   If the Underpainting palette is not already visible choose Window > Underpainting.

5   Increase the Saturation slider in the Underpainting palette from 0% to about 50%. See the effect in your image. The goal is to warm the image up and boost the color saturation.

6   If you like the effect choose Apply in the Underpainting palette.

7   Choose File > Save As, or use keyboard shortcut Shift-Cmd-S (Mac)/Shift-Ctrl-S (PC).

8   Save as a flat RGB TIFF file with name "ProjectName-05-eqlzsat.tif."

Get Rid of Photographic Grain

Smart Blur blurs the image while maintaining edges. It can be useful in suppressing grain in a photo. In the Underpainting palette move the Smart Blur slider to about 15%. It may take some time for the effect to be applied—it is a memory intensive effect. The benefit of applying Smart Blur is that it can avoid you accidentally having photo grain showing through in a painting. On the other hand it reduces the precision of the source information you have to work from and degrades your source image. Additionally, photo grain can sometimes be a good texture to keep and take advantage of.

At this stage, having completed the preparation of your source image for painting, you are ready to begin the painting process.

5

Painting From Photos II— Brushwork

Setting the Scene

In the previous chapter you prepared your source image for painting, starting with the capture of your image in the camera, and then with continued composition and refinement of your image in the computer, making use of both Adobe Photoshop and Corel Painter. Now the fun starts— it's time to paint! For the whole of this chapter you will be working exclusively in the world of Corel Painter. The brushwork I refer to in the title of this chapter is digital brushwork. The next chapter, Chapter 6 "Painting From Photos III—Completion," includes mention of post-print painting, which, of course, is also brushwork.

There is still some preparation to do connected with the workflow within Painter. You will begin with creating a "small-BIG" arrangement that mirrors the layout of a traditional artist working from photographic reference on a large canvas. My intention here is to provide you with a flexible and effective structure from which you can improvise and diverge. There are many choices along the way, and I endeavor to point some of them out as we go along. The guidelines and steps I share are not intended to be rigid rules, but simply ideas for you to play with. I encourage you to always experiment and take risks.

Two Themes

There are two overall themes to this chapter: general to detail, and viva variety.

1. General to Detail

Start general with big, bold, rough brushwork and then work towards selective detail using smaller, more precise, brushwork.

2. Viva Variety

Generate variations of your image and continually vary the hue, saturation, value, size, thickness, direction, structure and texture of your brushstrokes within your painting, whilst carefully observing your subject and being conscious, aware and intentional in all you do.

The image details shown here (Figures 5.1 and 5.2) illustrate the results of applying these two themes.

Three Challenges

Photographs present three significant challenges for painting.

Figure 5.1 *Waterfall*—detail showing the variety and richness of brushwork used to depict the effect of light reflecting from, and refracting through, the water.

Figure 5.2 *Generations*—detail showing variations of color, tone and texture in the shadow areas.

1. Too Much Detail

Photographs are usually full of detail that is very tempting to reproduce in a painting. Ironically a painting may be all the more powerful and beautiful when we include less precise detail, not more. Often a photograph has a large depth of field where much of the scene is in sharp focus, which again is a temptation to reproduce in a painting. By contrast a painting gives us a golden opportunity to be much more selective about what is in focus and to narrow down the depth of field, producing an effect closer to the narrow depth of field and limited focal region that human vision has.

The approach I share here starts with using big, bold, general brushstrokes to rapidly generate a fairly abstract "muck-up" underpainting. This approach distances us from the detail and helps us address the "too much detail" challenge.

2. Too Easy to Stick with Photo Color

Besides the temptation to include too much detail, the other temptation is to stick with the colors in the photo and not dare to be more adventurous. Part of the challenge with color is, ironically, that Painter makes it so easy to paint from a photo with the photo color. All the cloning brushes and effects in Painter allow you to make brush strokes which follow the color of your source image. Cloning in Painter is an immensely powerful tool but it can also become constrictive.

After going over my general "painting from photos" workflow in this and the subsequent chapter, I then focus in Chapter 7 on "going for it with color."

3. So Familiar I Don't Need to Look

The familiarity we have with the subject matter of the photograph, whether it be a person's face or a recognizable inanimate object, presents a surprisingly tough challenge. This familiarity is used by our powerful visual perception system to bypass the extra mental processing needed for accurate observation and interpretation of the color and tonal relationships and shapes we see. Instead, our visual perception system makes assumptions based on what we already know and are familiar with. Although it is an efficient way to work from a survival point of view (quick assessment of friend or foe, flight or fight, predator or prey) it makes painting what we see much more difficult. When I am painting from photographic reference I am continuously detaching myself from the "what it is" and instead looking at the source image as an abstract pattern of interlocking shapes of contrasting colors and tones. It is those shapes, and their relationships with one another, that I am continuously trying to depict in my choice of brush stroke color and tone.

Whilst Painter offers the powerful tools of Clone Color, where a brush uses the color from a source image, and Tracing Paper, where a source image shows through in a destination image, neither stops our natural subconscious familiarity with our subject getting in the way of accurate observation. Accurate observation can be helped by learning to draw, which I recommend for anyone, and by turning your source photograph upside down, which disconnects us from being attached to what we know things are, such as noses, mouths, and so on, and allows us to see better, and thus paint better, what is actually there in the image, such as lights, darks, colors and shapes. Betty Edwards' book *The New Drawing on the Right Side of the Brain* is full of exercises you can try out (in Painter or with traditional media) that help in this regard.

The Upside Down Option

If you haven't yet tried painting from an upside down photograph then have a go.

1 With your source image open in Painter, choose Canvas > Rotate Canvas > 180. This turns your image upside down.
2 Choose Shift-Cmd-S/Shift-Ctrl-S (File > Save As).
3 Save your image with "orig180" added in the notes section at the end of the file name.

The remaining instructions in this chapter are identical whether you have turned your source photograph upside down or not. If you do work from an upside down source photograph, I recommend you continue to do so for as much of the painting process as possible, and only rotate your source and working images back to the "right way up" in the final refinement stages.

Set Up The "small-BIG" Arrangement

The "small-BIG" arrangement of your source and working images allows you to conveniently work on your working image while maintaining visual reference to your source image at all times. It is the virtual equivalent of taping a small photo to the top left of your canvas. The "small-BIG" arrangement is simple, powerful and empowering. Essentially I zoom out (reduce the magnification) of my source image and place it in the upper left of my screen and then I place a larger magnification of the current working image on the right of my screen. Here's the detailed step-by-step procedure.

Small Source Image on Upper Left

1   With your source image open in Painter, and saved with a P-V-N name in an appropriately named project folder, click the Tab key to hide the palettes.

2   Click and drag the title bar of the source image window so that the top left corner of the source image window is tucked neatly into the top left corner of the Painter desktop (arrow 1 in Figure 5.3).

3   Drag the bottom right corner of your source image window frame downwards until it touches the bottom of your screen, and to the left until the source image window occupies approximately 20–25% of the total screen width (arrow 2 in Figure 5.3). Use a smaller percentage if you're working on a large monitor.

4   Choose Window > Zoom to Fit, or the keyboard shortcut Cmd-0 (Mac)/Ctrl-0 (PC), where "0" is the numeral zero.

5   Drag the Scale slider, located in the lower left of the source image window frame, slightly to the left to reduce the display magnification of the source image such that a small section of window background shows on left and right of the source image (arrow 3 in Figure 5.3).

6   Hold the Space bar down, which temporarily turns the cursor into the Grabber tool, while you drag in the source image upwards towards the top of its window frame (arrow 4 in Figure 5.3).

Big Working Image on Right

1   Choose File > Clone. This generates a duplicate copy of your source image. The copy automatically has "Clone of" added to the beginning of the file name and the source image automatically becomes the current clone source (see the check mark next to the source image file name under File > Clone Source). The source image will remain assigned to be the current clone source until you select another image as clone source, use a pattern or close the source file. The clone copy image is your working image, that is, the canvas that you paint on. The benefit of

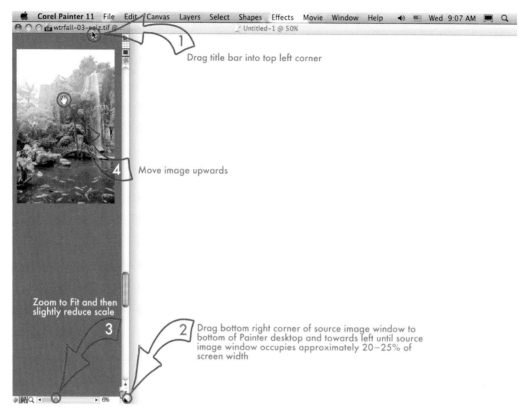

Figure 5.3 Setting up a small source image on the upper left of the Painter desktop.

using the Clone command to generate the working image, besides the convenience of instantly having a copy of your source image and the establishment of a clone relationship between the source and clone copy images, is that your working image is always exactly the same size as your source image. In other words this is a helpful technique for establishing a template.

2 Click and drag the title bar of your working (clone copy) image window and move the image window so the top left of the window is neatly aligned along the top of the screen and the left side of the working image window frame is overlapping and covering up the right side of the source image window frame.

3 Drag the bottom right corner of your working image window down and to the right until it is neatly tucked into the bottom right corner of your computer screen (Figure 5.4).

4 Choose Tab so the palettes show again.

5 Hold the Space bar while you move the source and working images to positions where they are completely unobstructed by palettes. Drag the Scale slider in the lower left of the working image window frame slightly to the right to zoom in and maximize the display size of the working image. Make sure you can see all edges of both the source image and the working image (Figure 5.5). Adjust the palette arrangement and Scale sliders as needed.

Figure 5.4 Setting up a big working image on the right of the Painter desktop.

Choose Between Many Paths

At this stage you are at a crossroads, with many possible paths of where to go with your working image. Some of the possible choices you may wish to consider include the following:

(a) Utilize Window > Auto-Painting with Smart Stroke Painting and Smart Settings checked and using an interesting brush such as Artists > Impressionists with Clone Color selected.

(b) Apply Effects > Surface Control > Woodcut to generate a poster print style variation.

(c) Leave the photograph in the working image canvas and paint over it by hand (as opposed to Auto-Painting).

(d) Choose Select > Select All and then Delete (Mac)/Backspace (PC), leaving a blank white canvas (unless the canvas paper color has been set to another color) which you might use with Tracing Paper and for making pencil/chalk/pen and ink style drawings or water color style paintings. If you know in advance you want this option then you could use File > Quick Clone instead of File > Clone.

(e) Fill the working image canvas with a uniform color or gradient fill, and then paint over that. The uniform color can be picked from the Colors, Mixer or Color Sets palettes, or you

Figure 5.5 The "small-BIG" arrangement with palettes showing (the arrangement of palettes is a slight modification of the JeremyBasic palette arrangement in the Jeremy_P11_Wkspc_1 included on the Resource Disc with this book and available, along with more brushes and videos, at PaintboxJ.com).

can use the Dropper tool and pick the color from within the photograph itself. A gradient can be chosen using the Gradient Selector in the Gradients palette (Window > Library Palettes > Gradients). I like to use the Two-Point gradient with the Main and Additional colors in the Colors palette. I orientate the gradient by moving the red dot in the gradient orientation preview. You can fill your canvas with either the current color or gradient by choosing Edit > Fill, or Cmd-F (Mac)/Ctrl-F (PC).

The five options listed above are not mutually exclusive choices. I will sometimes purposely generate a series of variations based on a common source image and then mix them together at a later stage. The beauty of working in Painter is that it makes it so easy to follow multiple creative paths, generate many variations on a theme, and then mix and blend elements of the different variations together in a final composite. No path is a waste or a dead-end. Every path expands the realms of possibilities, even if you end up not using the result.

What is Clone Color?

To understand what Clone Color is we must first understand the concept of cloning in Painter. For many people "cloning" is associated with making identical copies, whether of objects, animals or humans. In Painter cloning is a relationship between a source and a destination, which allows certain brushes (those from the Cloners category, and brushes from other categories when the Clone Color icon is activated in the Colors palette) to derive color from whatever the current clone source is and apply it into a destination. You can see what the current clone source is at any time by looking at File > Clone Source. There will be a check mark by the current clone source, which by default is the current pattern.

The destination image can be the same as the clone source image, as in point-to-point cloning, where you clone from one place in an image into another place in the same image. There is a dedicated Rubber Stamp tool (shortcut is the Apostrophe key) specially for this type of operation. It can be found seven icons down on left of the Toolbox sharing a fly-out with the Cloner tool. You can set the clone source start position when working with the Rubber Stamp tool by clicking once holding down the Option or Alt key. You will see a green dot with a "1" above it, signifying the clone start position.

The clone operation in Painter (File > Clone) generates a flat duplicate image of your current active image, exactly the same size as the file you cloned from, with "Clone of" added to be beginning of the file name of the duplicate image. The Clone operation automatically sets the source file you cloned from to be assigned as the current clone source. Your clone copy is the destination image. The Clone Source setting is only temporary and is not a property of either the source or clone copy image. If you close Painter and return to it later and reopen the source file and the clone copy file, the source file will not automatically be the clone source. You will have to manually reset it to be that (using the File > Clone Source menu).

The File > QuickClone Operation does a number of operations in one. These are defined Preferences > General. By default the QuickClone will duplicate the source image (creating a Clone Copy), set the source image to be clone source, clear the duplicate image, turn on Tracing Paper (which allows you to see the clone source superimposed over the destination image, provided they are the same size) and select the last used Cloner brush.

Thus, in the context of painting from photographs, it is very useful to make a clone copy of your source photo and be able to paint in that clone with brushes that use Clone Color. Such brushes pick color from the corresponding location in the source image.

Two Quick Paths to Generate Variations: Auto-Painting & Woodcut

In the interests of experimentation and exploration, I suggest you initially try out the Auto-Painting (Figure 5.6) and the Woodcut effect (Figures 5.7 and 5.8), keeping them as variations, saving the stages and results with the same P-V-N file naming system, and maintaining the system of sequential version numbers. These techniques offer two easy and fast ways to generate variations for later use. After applying each technique, make another clone copy from your source image using the "small-BIG" arrangement. The underlying principle is to always work on a clone copy working image, not directly on the source image.

Figure 5.6 The result of Auto-Painting with Smart Stroke Painting and Smart Settings checked and using the Artists > Impressionists brush variant with the Clone Color icon active in the Colors palette.

Three Slower Paths with More Heart and Soul

While these two fast automatic techniques, Auto-Painting and the Woodcut effect, may produce interesting results, they do not offer the heart, soul, unique individuality or level of variation possible when you apply brush strokes by hand (with the use of a Wacom tablet and pen). For that reason my main focus in this book is on the slower techniques of applying brush strokes and effects by hand, rather than the faster techniques in which the computer automatically applies brush strokes or effects, or filters through mathematical computation. I much prefer paint-by-hand to paint-by-machine. Besides looking better, it is also more fun! To explain and illustrate my slower, paint-by-hand approach, I shall use three different case studies:

- In *Generations* (Figure 4.2, or on the web at www.jeremysutton.com/generations.html) I painted over the photo in the working image. In some sections of the final painting you can still see small areas of photo grain showing through, which is one of the disadvantages of painting over the photo (look carefully at Figure 5.2). I chose to leave the photograph in the

Figure 5.7 Applying the Effects > Surface Control > Woodcut effect to the *Waterfall* image.

working image canvas when I started painting this since I wanted to keep much of the photograph as it was. However, in retrospect looking back at the result, I see that keeping the photograph there resulted in a tighter, more conservative and photographic end result. Whilst I share this example as one of the case studies in this book, my overall advice is to initially let go of photographic detail completely.

• In "Waterfall" (Figure 4.1, or on the web at www.jeremysutton.com/waterfall.html) I cleared the working image canvas to white and then built up the painting from scratch on that white canvas. I chose to start with a blank white canvas since I wanted to begin the painting with a "nod" to traditional Chinese calligraphy. Ultimately I ended up painting over the entire canvas and covering up almost all my early black on white calligraphic brush marks. Having history buried within your canvas is part of what builds up a rich and interesting surface, and contributes to the painterly quality of your end-result. That is also why I emphasize not "undoing," always moving forward and being committed to your marks and your process. This is an immensely empowering principle.

• In a third example that I share here, *Dawn* (Figure 5.9, or on the web at www.jeremysutton. com/dawnhampton.html), my portrait of dancer, performer and teacher Dawn Hampton, I

Figure 5.8 The result of applying the Woodcut effect to the *Waterfall* image.

initially filled the working image canvas with a mid-tone color. There is a long tradition in oil painting of starting with a mid-tone "ground" (background) on the canvas, which this option emulates. There was so much warmth in Dawn's personality, and in the clothing and surroundings captured in the source photograph, that I wanted to use a warm background color to imbue the painting with a warm glow. I also wanted to convey Dawn's energy with colorful, big, bold brush strokes and that is much easier to do against a colored, non-photographic background. An additional benefit of starting with a mid-tone color background is

Figure 5.9 My portrait of inspirational singer, dancer, performer and teacher Dawn Hampton.

that it makes it easy to paint both highlights and shadows, whereas it is difficult to show a highlight against a white canvas or a shadow against a dark canvas.

Part of the reason I illustrate my paint-by-hand process with these three examples is to help give you a sense of the freedom you have, and show how different the paths were for these three paintings. The paintings *Generations* and *Waterfall* are both subjects of video tutorials on PaintboxJ.com and, if you are interested to see my actual brush strokes unfolding on the screen, that's the place to go. There's no substitute for seeing paint in motion when it comes to communicating the freedom, spontaneity and flow of my creative process.

Another reason I am using three case studies in parallel is to avoid sharing a single specific recipe which may then appear as if I am suggesting that is the "right" way to do things. There are no "right" and "wrong" ways to do things—simply choices with consequences. You are the judge of what works best for you. I recommend that you start off by trying out all five options, a through e, with a common source image and compare the results for yourself. Treat this as a research project. You may end up wishing to mix "n" match elements of the different results to make a final composite.

Subsequently, for future projects, you can then evaluate what technique, or combination of techniques, feels most appropriate. I rarely know at the beginning of a project exactly how I am going to proceed. If I do "know," then it is almost certain that by the end of the project whatever I had initially planned has been departed from many times! You can see from the examples shown in this chapter how dramatically my paintings may transform during the creative process. It is useful to set a vision and have a plan, but it is just as important to be flexible, able to let go of your plans and assumptions at any moment in the process, to be open to serendipity, to expect and accept imperfections, and to respond to the unexpected with spontaneous improvisation. This applies on the macroscopic level, that is, with the overall direction of your painting, as well as on the microscopic level, with being able to let go of, and paint over, parts of your painting you may be attached to. Enough philosophizing—let's get painting!

On Your Marks, Get Set...

Once you have chosen whether to start with leaving the photo in the working image, or clearing it to white or filling with a uniform color or color gradient, choose File > Save As, Cmd-Shift-S (Mac)/Ctrl-Shift-S (PC), and save the starting working image, continuing the P-V-N file naming system described in Chapter 3. Make sure the name begins with the short project name, that it has the next sequential two-digit version number, and indicates in the notes part of the P-V-N file name whether the working image is filled with the photo, white or a color (I usually note what

Figure 5.10 The *Generations* working image with the photograph left in the background.

Figure 5.11 The *Waterfall* working image after choosing Select > Select All and then Delete (Mac)/Backspace (PC).

color). A quick and easy way to get rid of the "Clone of " that is automatically added at the beginning of a clone copy file name is, in the Save As dialog window browser, to simply click on the name of the last saved version listed in the project folder where you are saving the files. This then automatically changes the current file name to the one you click on, and then you adjust the version number and notes appropriately. This works on both Macs and PCs. Once you start painting use the notes section of the file name to keep track of the brushes you use.

As you continue to work, remember to *regularly* (at least every 10 minutes) do a Save As and strictly maintain the P-V-N file naming convention throughout the painting process. This is very important! If you were sitting in one of my workshops I would be coming around every five minutes and saying, "Time for a Save As!," or "If you haven't done a Save As in the last two seconds then it's time to do one now!" You may have experienced this first hand, in which case you know I am not exaggerating:-) If you are new to my system, please let me reassure you that saving regularly and maintaining the P-V-N naming system makes a huge difference to your creative empowerment and what you can achieve in Painter. Please try it out and see for yourself. For the sake of brevity and clarity I shall not be repeating this throughout the book, or including the regular "Save As's" in every step-by-step instruction. It will be assumed you have read this paragraph and are following this system throughout every project.

As a painting develops it undergoes continuous transformations, growing from abstract infancy, through the "ugly stage," to refined maturity. This process of transformation, which may

Figure 5.12 The *Dawn Hampton* working image after clicking in the image with the Dropper tool to select a mid-tone color, and then choosing Edit > Fill, or Cmd-F (Mac)/Ctrl-F (PC), and filling with the current color. Note on this project I began with the source image upside down. To turn your image upside down choose Canvas > Rotate Canvas > 180.

encompass many intermediate stages and passages, can be roughly broken down into an initial phase that I refer to as the "muck up," the early abstract underpainting stage, followed by the "four Rs" phase—the main bulk of the painting time which is spent in repeated iterative cycles of revealing, refining, reviewing and resolving. In the remainder of this chapter I shall explain these two phases of the painting process.

Start Abstract—The "Muck Up" Stage

Start with large, loose brush strokes and don't worry about detail at all. There will be plenty of time for working in details later. Beginnings are about:

i   the big picture;

ii rapidly establishing on your canvas the main shapes of lights, darks and colors, and the relationships between them;

iii creating a lively backdrop which focuses on the abstract forms of your composition and serves as an underpainting on which you can develop as detailed a depiction of your subject as you wish, capturing the raw energy, mood, movement and atmosphere; and

iv painting loosely and with gusto!

I refer to this abstract early stage of the painting process as the "muck up" stage to convey that it doesn't have to look pretty and that it is created rapidly with looseness and flow. The "muck up" stage should be able to stand alone as an abstract, even while being loosely based on the source photo. My only concern with using the term "muck up" is that it may inadvertently indicate a chaotic randomness to the way brush strokes are applied. In fact the "muck up" stage involves intense observation, focus, care and intention with every brush stroke.

Art & Entropy

The word "entropy" is derived from the Greek for "a turning towards." The scientific concept of "entropy" can be loosely interpreted as the tendency for any closed system to turn towards increasing disorder, uncertainty or chaos, and towards the homogeneous distribution of energy across all possible energy states of a system. In a closed system, when there is an increase in order in one part of the system, there is an associated increase in disorder and chaos somewhere else in the system. Thus order is always balanced by disorder, and the two coexist simultaneously. We can think of this as a universal law of harmony that balances the two opposites.

An analogy to entropy in a painting is the level of abstraction or disorder. As we build up a painting, and especially in the early "muck up" stage, we need to be able to tolerate, even embrace, a certain amount of disorder, uncertainty and chaos.

As our painting proceeds into the "four Rs" stage of revealing, refining, reviewing and resolving, we start to progressively bring more and more order and, consequently, meaning, to the painting at a macroscopic level, that is, what the painting looks like when you step back and look at it from a distance. At a brush stroke ("microscopic") level the painting is still abstract and chaotic.

In painting, abstraction and representation coexist simultaneously, just like disorder and order in the universal law of entropy. Every representational painting, that is, a painted flat surface that represents something three-dimensional, is an illusion. When we stand back from a representational painting and look at it from a distance (that is, look at it from a "macroscopic" level), the illusion works. Our visual perception system interprets the brush marks in terms of representing something which they are not. When we walk right up to a painting and analyze the brush strokes in detail ("microscopic" level) they are quite abstract.

If we are not careful and intentional in the way we apply brush strokes and blend paint on our canvas, there will be a tendency towards "meaningless mush." This is the art equivalent of the homogeneous distribution of energy across all possible energy states of a system.

As artists we can draw upon the connections between art and entropy to help us be aware of, tolerate and control the relationship between order and disorder and between abstraction and representation in our painting process.

The main guidelines to creating the initial "muck up" are as follows:

1 Start by choosing a brush with bold textured brush strokes and making it large enough that you are not tempted to get into detail too soon. There are too many brushes to name that can work as good "muck up" brushes. Try out the brushes in JeremyFaves2. In the three examples shown here you see the use of quite different brushes. Whatever you choose to start with, I recommend you change brushes several times to get variety in types of brush marks.

2 Before you make your first brush strokes, look intensely at your source image. Half close your eyes and carefully observe how the darks and lights vary and contrast in your source image. Start putting some brush strokes into your working image that show you roughly where the lightest lights and darkest darks are, and that indicate the main shapes and lines of movement.

3 Use your own color choices, not Clone Color. Pick colors that evoke the mood of your subject, not just what colors happen to be in the photo. By departing from the photo color you'll end up with a much more interesting painting. In the examples shown here look at the similarities and differences between the source image and muck up colors.

4 Rapidly make large, expressive, energetic brush strokes that describe where the lightest lights and darkest darks are, and that follow the basic forms and movement of your source image. Vary your colors regularly. Avoid too much uniformity as you fill the canvas.

5 Continually look back and forth between your source image and your working image as you paint. Make every mark intentional, not random.

6 Don't use the Undo command, or be tentative or concerned that you may not have the "right" brush or that your brush strokes may not be "right." Don't get too attached to any marks or try to get anything looking perfect. This is about rapidly filling your canvas with loose brush strokes.

7 Add a variety of types of brushes and brush marks. You can add some narrower crisp, clean and distinct accent strokes but don't get into any details of your subject at this stage. You can apply brushes that blend and distort (for instance Distortion > Pinch and Jeremy Faves 2 > Artists Palette Knife). Avoid repetition of the same brush stroke and color across the whole canvas. Continually think variety...

The whole "muck up" paint process need not take longer than 10 to 15 minutes. If you go beyond 15 minutes there is a chance the abstract "muck up" may become a homogeneous "mush up" instead!

Reveal, Refine, Review and Resolve—The "Four Rs" Stage

We have our "muck up" phase completed and have created a lively backdrop on which to develop detail. The next step is to selectively reveal some of our main subject, refine and emphasize select details, review what still needs resolving in the painting and then act to resolve it. The process of reveal, refine, review and resolve is an iterative one that is repeated many, many times. Painting is problem solving and this cycle of reveal, refine, review and resolve is analogous

Figure 5.13 The *Generations* muck up shown here when I was applying JeremyGuestFaves4 (also in JeremyFaves2) > Sherron's Blender Wood.

to the way a scientist repeatedly refines, reviews and adjusts their theory to fit the results of empirical observations.

When I analyze the time I spend on different aspects of my painting process I find that typically I spend 90% of my painting time on the reveal, refine, review and resolve portion of the process. You can see this reflected in the proportion of versions that are part of the "muck up" phase versus the "four Rs" phase:

- *Generations*: Five versions "muck up"—forty-five versions reveal, refine, review and resolve;
- *Waterfall*: Three versions "muck up"—forty-four versions reveal, refine, review and resolve;
- *Dawn Hampton*: Three versions "muck up"—twenty-three versions reveal, refine, review and resolve.

The take away from this information is to be patient and persevere. Don't expect the painting to suddenly and magically work and be completed. It can take time. The process of refining and resolving an artwork can take days, months or even years. In some senses it never ends—when I look at a painting I made years ago I often see things that I still want to change and resolve.

Figure 5.14 The *Waterfall* muck up created using Calligraphy > Dry Ink. This "muck up" is more related to drawing than painting. This image later undergoes a complete transformation, as you'll see.

Reveal the Subject Through Limited Cloning

The first challenge after creating your "muck up" is how to go about depicting your subject without simply covering all the wonderful colorful and energetic brush marks you have just made. One answer is to selectively reveal your subject with a combination of a little clone color for positioning and scale reference, and mostly non-clone color. You can also choose to avoid Clone Color altogether and allow your painting to have a more freehand feel. That is a stylistic choice that is in your hands as the artist and that you may wish to experiment with. Here are some general tips to get you going on this stage of the painting process.

1   Reduce your brush size to a scale where you can start defining the main shapes of your subject and compositional elements. Be selective. This is where "less is more" (see the sidebar).
2   Make use of your full screen area. Zoom in, using Window > Zoom In, or Cmd-+ (Mac)/Ctrl-+ (PC), with both the source and working images, to an area where you wish to reveal more details in your subject. You can click on the Navigation icon (looks like a pair of binoculars) at the bottom left of the window frame to locate where your zoomed in view is vis-à-vis the complete image, and to move around within the image. Periodically choose Window > Zoom to Fit, or Cmd-0 (Mac)/Ctrl-0 (PC), and zoom out to see your whole image.

Figure 5.15 The Dawn Hampton muck up in which I used Sherron's Blender Wood and David's Sui Rui, both variants in the JeremyGuestFaves4 (and also in the JeremyFaves2) category.

3 Choose brushes whose texture and look you like and feel is appropriate to the subject.

4 Activate the Clone Color icon in the Colors palette (keyboard shortcut "U") so the brush starts picking up color from the source image. Look at File > Clone Source to make sure your source image is the clone source. If not, manually set it to be Clone Source. For some brushes, such as the Sargent Brush and Impressionist brush, in Clone mode you will see a cross-hair in the source image showing where the color is derived from. This can be very useful. Not all cloning brushes show the cross-hair (for instance, many of the Cloners category brushes do not).

5 Make enough brush dabs and strokes in your working image muck up to help define where the main structures of your composition are. You will see that you bring in color from your source image. Don't bring back too much detail. These marks are for reference. You may notice how dull the clone colors are that you bring into your image compared with the non-clone colors you've added and built up.

"Less is More"

One of the biggest challenges of working from photographs is the strong temptation to include too much detail just because it's there in the original photograph. Oscar-winning sound and picture editor Walter Murch, who worked with Francis Ford Coppola on the film *Apocalypse Now*, explains eloquently in his book *In the Blink of an Eye: A Perspective on Film Editing* (Silman-James Press, 1995) why less detail engages the viewers' imagination more than too much detail:

> You may not always succeed, but attempt to produce the greatest effect in the viewer's mind by the least number of things on screen. Why? Because you want to do only what is necessary to engage the imagination of the audience. Suggestion is always more effective than exposition. Past a certain point, the more effort you put into wealth of detail, the more you encourage the audience to become spectators rather than participants.

As you work at this stage of your painting see how little detail you can bring back into the painting from the source photograph to evoke the subject.

Here are examples of the three case study paintings showing how I began to reveal the subjects and define details.

Figure 5.16 Bringing out details in *Generations* using the Artists > Sargent Brush. Note the use of zoomed in views with both the source and working images, and the use of a relatively small brush size.

Figure 5.17 The *Waterfall* went through many stages of development. Prior to the stage caught here, the Tinting > Basic Round Brush had been used to create soft diffuse color and the Artists > Impressionist Brush had been used for more detailed work. You see in this figure the Cloners > Oil Brush, which has a slight Impasto effect, being applied to define the bridge.

Refine Selected Details Through Careful Attention to Tone and Contrasts

Once you have mapped out some critical portions of your subject stick to non-clone color. At that stage further reduce the size of your brushes and focus on observing carefully in your source image the exact tonal relationships, shapes and contrasts between adjacent blocks of color in regions of your composition that you wish to emphasize and draw attention to. Then work to reproduce, or even exaggerate, those relationships and contrasts with your paint in your working image. This process involves a lot of looking back and forth between your source image and your working image. It is helpful for both images to be zoomed in so you can easily observe the details. It can be helpful from time to time to choose Window > Underpainting and take the Saturation slider all the way to the left with both the source and working images. This allows you to compare them in Desaturated mode and focus more on the lights and darks. Click the Reset button in the Underpainting palette to return to full color.

Figure 5.18 The same David's Sui Rui variant used in the muck up stage is now being used, with smaller brush size and intermittent use of clone color, to bring more definition to the face.

Review What is Working and Not Working

1   Periodically step away from your painting and take a short break. I suggest you do this at least every 20 minutes, if not more frequently.

2   When you return from your break choose Tab (Window > Hide Palettes).

3   Choose Window > Screen Mode Toggle, or Cmd-M (Mac)/Ctrl-M (PC).

4   Choose Window > Zoom to Fit, or Cmd-0 (Mac)/Ctrl-0 (PC).

5   Choose Window > Zoom Out, or Cmd-"-" (Mac)/Ctrl-"-" (PC).

6   Stand back from your computer and look at your painting.

7   Ask yourself what is working and not working. This is an important time to step back and consider the big picture. It is easy to get lost in details and lose sight of the overall composition. Try zooming out until the working image is the size of a postage stamp. Does it work well as a composition at that small scale? Are the lights and darks clearly discernible at that scale?

Figure 5.19 Using a very small Sherron's Blender Wood variant to bring out tonal detail in *Generations*.

Figure 5.20 Using JeremyOwnFaves4 > Jeremy's Smooth Oily to define and refine contrasts in *Waterfall*.

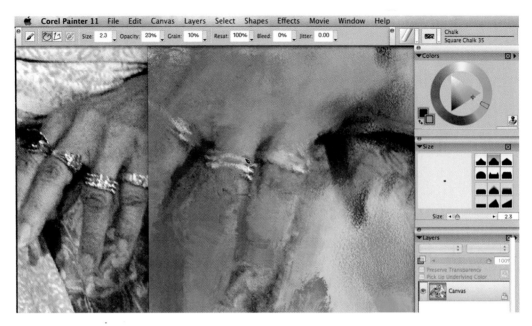

Figure 5.21 Using a small Chalks > Square Chalk 35 to add color to one of Dawn's rings in *Dawn Hampton*. Note that the source and working images are now the right way up (achieved using Canvas > Rotate Canvas > 180) since at this stage of going into detail it felt easier and more efficient.

Resolve What is Not Working

1 Choose Window > Screen Mode Toggle, or Cmd-M (Mac)/Ctrl-M (PC).

2 Choose Tab (Window > Show Palettes).

3 Return to painting and resolving what you observed wasn't working (Figures 5.19, 5.20 and 5.21). As with the refining process, look back and forth between the source image and your working image, and continuously compare tonal relationships. Periodically use the Underpainting palette Saturation slider to test how your painting is working in grayscale.

Bootstrap Cloning

If you are finding that you are getting too photographic or are being tempted to use too much clone color, one solution is to use one of your earlier painted versions of your image as the clone source instead of the source photograph. I call this technique "bootstrap cloning." Doing so will enliven your colors and ensure you don't lose the painterliness of the image. The Cloners > Camel Oil Cloner is a good brush for cloning detail with a smooth oily look when bootstrapping.

Return-to-Photo Layer Technique

Alternatively you may find that you want to get back more photographic detail. One way to do that is to use the return-to-photo layer technique. Here are the steps.

1   Generate a new transparent layer either by choosing the New Layer icon in the Layers palette, or Layers > New, or Shift-Cmd-N (Mac)/Shift-Ctrl-N (PC). Make sure Preserve Transparency is unchecked.

2   Choose Cloners > Soft Cloner.

3   Set brush to low opacity.

4   Paint in your detail areas into this Soft Clone layer.

5   Apply a good oily brush such as the Cloners > Camel Oil Cloner or Artists > Sargent Brush or Jeremy Faves 2 > Den's Oil Funky Chunky onto the Soft Clone layer. These oily brushes do not work on transparent layers but do work on imagery already on a layer.

6   Choose Save As and save the file as a RIFF file.

7   Choose Layers > Drop All.

8   Now you can apply blending and distortion brushes to blend everything together.

Generating Graphic Variation Using Composite Method Layer Technique

This is a technique you can use to generate a variation with photographic detail from a rough "muck up" painting. This variation can then be used as a clone source for selectively cloning into a layer, as described in the Mix It In section later in this chapter (page 136).

1   Click in your source image so it is the active image in Painter.

2   Choose Select > All, or Cmd-A (Mac)/Ctrl-A (PC).

3   Choose Edit > Copy, or Cmd-C (Mac)/Ctrl-C (PC).

4   Holding the Space bar down click once in your working image (or an earlier "muck up" stage). This centers the image.

5   Let go of the Space bar.

6   Choose Edit > Paste, or Cmd-Shift-V (Mac)/Ctrl-Shift-V (PC). This will paste in the source image as a layer over the painted image.

7   Experiment with the different composite methods (Gel, Colorize, etc.) in the Layers palette. The Composite Methods pop-up menu is at the top left of the Layers palette and initially says Default. Composite methods are the Painter equivalent of layer blending modes in Photoshop. Don't be surprised if many of the composite methods give results that look awful! One or two may give you an interesting effect you like, or a portion of which you may wish to use.

8   When you see an effect you like choose File Save As and save as a RIFF file. I find that Overlay and Hard Light composite methods are the two I use the most.

Pick Up Color From Within Your Painting

As you paint it can be helpful to pick color from within your working image using the Dropper tool (keyboard shortcut "D"), maybe altering the saturation and value slightly. When you have a non-clone brush active, the Option (Mac)/Alt (PC) key turns your current Brush tool cursor into a Dropper tool. However, when the current brush is a Cloner Brush, or any other brush with the Clone Color icon active in the Colors palette, then the same shortcut becomes the shortcut for resetting the clone start position, used for point-to-point cloning. Since it is so easy to accidentally reset the clone start position when you mean to select the Dropper tool, I suggest you use the "D" key to change your tool to the Dropper tool when you need it and the "B" key to return to the Brush tool afterwards. If you do accidentally reset the clone start position, go to File > Clone Source and reset the clone source back to the source file you want it to be. If you find the registration (positioning) of your cloning is offset, choose the Cloners > Soft Cloner and click the Restore Default Variant icon (left of the Property Bar).

Smaller, Finer Detail over Bigger, Rougher Brushstrokes

As you paint, continuously look for ways to add depth and richness to your painting by varying your brushes, your brush size, your colors and tone. Consider overlaying accent strokes and dabs with strong color relationships to the colors behind them, for instance either complementary colors from the opposite side of the Hue Ring (Painter's color wheel in the Colors palette) or analogous colors from adjacent positions around the Hue Ring. Look at the ways painters, ranging from the French Impressionist Claude Monet to pop artist Andy Warhol, have used accent strokes and dabs to great effect.

Repeat the "Four Rs" Cycle

Iteratively Working Towards Completion

The "Four Rs" process described here is a continuous and repeating cycle. You will not complete your painting in one cycle of these steps but in many, many cycles, each one of which hones in on your vision for the painting and, usually, brings you closer to completion.

The Imperfect Process

The process of refining and resolving a painting is sometimes awkward and ugly! The painting process is one of "it's not working, it's not working, it's not working, it's not working..." followed by "...aah, that's it!" It is a bumpy and imperfect process. You may find your painting either veering towards too much detail and too much photo, or conversely veering away again into too much loose abstract brushwork. This awkwardness is part of the process so don't panic, get frustrated or give up. Just stay committed and work through the process. Please note the large number of versions that I went through in this phase of the creative process with the three examples used in this chapter.

This "four Rs" phase is not all plain sailing—there is often a lot of struggle. I think of myself as wrestling with the painting. It may sometimes feel like a fight, yet it is also a dance in which the painting is my partner and the subject is my music. If you persevere and work through the

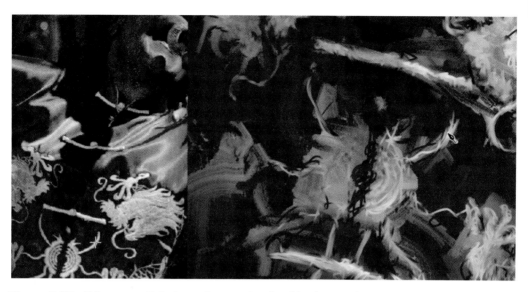

Figure 5.22 Using a small Artists > Sargent Brush with Clone Color and palettes hidden, I paint the clothing detail in *Generations*.

Figure 5.23 Adding small dabs of color onto foliage in *Waterfall* using the Artists > Sargent Brush.

awkward and ugly stages, and if you accept that imperfection is not only part of the process but adds richness to the end result, then I am sure you'll be amazed at what you end up creating.

Film Director Francis Ford Coppola expressed these sentiments, and described the roughness of the creative process very eloquently in the following story he told when interviewed on National Public Radio's Forum program.

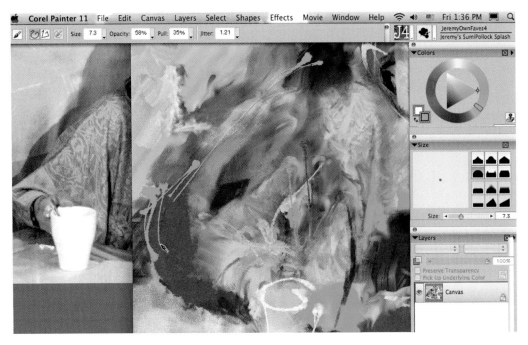

Figure 5.24 Applying accents strokes with JeremyOwnFaves4 (also in JeremyFaves2) > Jeremy's SumiPollock Splash in *Dawn Hampton*.

Something I always tell my kids, great films have as many flaws and bad things about them as bad films. I could take you through Citizen Kane, or any number of films, and just point out all the flaws and give notes on all that's wrong with them. The difference is the good films light up, the illusion works, so when you see them you're not looking at the flaws. What it tells me when someone sees a film and says I don't like that, or it gets bad reviews, the film didn't light up for them, so that you tend to only see the bad things.

I tell my kids it's the cigarette lighter theory: you have a cigarette lighter and that's your movie. You try to light it and you flick it and it doesn't light. Then you pull the wick out and do it and it doesn't light. Then you pour more fluid and you put too much and it doesn't light. You dry it off with a hairdryer and it doesn't light. Then you pull the wick out some more and all of a sudden it lights! And once it lights all the bad things that didn't have the conditions of lighting go away because it's lit. That's what a movie is like. You have this thing and it doesn't work. The audience comes out and they just talk about the bad things. But then you change it, you move it around, you move it here, you do this, and you tweak it a little. And when it lights all the bad things go away. They don't go away. But you don't look at them any more because you're lost in the illusion.

Mix It In—Combining Different Versions Together

We started this chapter with the exploration of some different options for working from a photograph, including the use of Auto-Painting and the Woodcut effect. Thus we generated some variations based on the same image. One possibility at your fingertips at any stage in the process is to mix from different stages or variations. This is analogous to the way a DJ may mix different parts of different songs together in a single composition—hence my use of the term "mix it in." (This is a more advanced technique and if you are new to Painter I suggest you leave this until you are completely familiar with the basic painting workflow described earlier.)

When applying any effect or filter to your image this "mix it in" technique is useful for subtle integration of the effect into your composition. Often an effect applied everywhere is overkill. You can, of course, always choose Edit > Fade, Shift-Cmd-F (Mac)/Shift-Ctrl-F (PC) immediately after applying any effect or brush stroke to fade it away anywhere between 100% and 0%. However, the "mix it in" technique gives you even more control than the Fade over how you introduce one image into another.

Here is the general methodology to follow for the "mix it in" technique:

1   Open all versions of your image you wish to mix together. These files should all have exactly the same number of pixels wide by high.

2   Set up your different versions in small, zoomed out display windows on the left of your Painter desktop (Figure 5.25). Although in theory you could have any number of different

Figure 5.25   With three different versions of *Waterfall* on the left, I chose to assign the Woodcut version to be the clone source. You can see here how important the file naming system is. If you had a very long project name in your file name you could not know which file is which in the Clone Source list.

versions open, in practice I find typically that three versions is about the maximum to work with at one time.

3 Choose the one version you are going to use as your main base image onto which you'll clone in portions of the other versions. Click on the chosen base image and make sure it is the currently active image in Painter. You can verify this by making sure the file name has a check mark beside it at the bottom of the Window menu.

4 Choose File > Clone and make a clone copy of the base image version.

5 Set that clone copy in a "BIG" arrangement on the right of your desktop (Figure 5.25), that is, zoomed in and with the edge of the canvas window neatly overlapping the different versions on the left and reaching to the upper right and bottom edges of your desktop.

6 Choose the Cloners > Soft Cloner brush variant in the Brush Selectors palette.

7 Make the brush size relatively large.

8 Choose File > Clone Source and select which version you wish to clone into the base image. Once you have selected that file name in the Clone Source list it will have a check mark beside it next time you look (Figure 5.25).

9 Click on the New Layer icon, third from the right in the row of icons at the bottom of the Layers palette (Figure 5.26). This generates a transparent new layer, "Layer 1." Make sure the Preserve Transparency checkbox is left unchecked.

10 Double click on the Layer 1 name and rename with a short descriptive name (Figure 5.27).

11 Now you can clone into the layer, using the Soft Cloner, from your chosen source (Figure 5.28).

12 At any time you can return to File > Clone Source, change the clone source, and paint from a different version into a new layer.

13 Painting in the layers allows you to adjust the opacity of each layer in the Layers list. You could also add a layer mask by clicking on the Create Layer Mask icon on the far right of the row of icons at the bottom of the Layers palette. Painting in black with, for instance, an

Figure 5.26 Clicking on the New Layer icon in the Layers list.

Figure 5.27 Rename the new layer by double clicking on its name in the Layers palette.

Figure 5.28 Apply Soft Clone brush strokes in the layer to mix the versions.

Figure 5.29 Painting in the layer mask with black Digital Airbrush to take away portions of the layer visibility.

Airbrush > Digital Airbrush (Figure 5.29), will make what is in the layer transparent and reveal what is underneath. Painting with white in the layer mask does the opposite, bringing back the layer visibility and concealing what is underneath.

Flatten

During the course of your painting process you may end up generating layers, depending on the brushes and techniques you use. An important workflow strategy is to end up flattening your image.

1   Before you flatten your image choose Save As and save the layered file in Painter RIFF file format. This preserves the editability of every layer.

2   Choose Layers > Drop All (also accessible under the Layers palette pop-up menu). This command will flatten all layers, provided there are no locked layers. Layers can be locked and unlocked simply by clicking on the lower right corner of the layer in the Layers list, immediately beneath the Layer icon that informs you what type of layer it is. You'll see a

padlock icon appear when the layer is locked. A locked layer is protected from accidental painting or moving around or changing of the composite method (equivalent of the blending modes in Photoshop). If you have a lot of layers it can be useful to lock the ones you do not wish to alter. When you wish to flatten an image make sure all the layers are unlocked.

3 Choose Save As and save the flat file in TIFF file format. This is now openable in all other programs that handle bitmap images, including Photoshop.

If you save a layered file in Painter using Photoshop (PSD) file format, the file will open, with the layers still present as layers, in Photoshop. However, there are certain special types of layers in Painter that will not be preserved in the Photoshop format. These include Digital Watercolor, Watercolor, Liquid Ink, Impasto, Mosaic and all the plug-in layers such as Liquid Metal and Kaleidoscope. Those that appear in the Layers list will be converted into default image layers. Certain composite methods will also change, such as Gel, which will be converted to Darken in Photoshop. Thus your image may end up looking quite different to what you intended unless you flatten the image first.

Besides the advantage of ensuring consistency with what you see in Photoshop, there is also another benefit to flattening your image at regular intervals and that is the ability to work into your entire image on the background canvas with blending and distortion brushes.

Next Step

The ideas, approach and techniques shared in this chapter are just scratching the surface of what it is possible to do when working from photographic reference in Painter. After trying these ideas go into other areas of the program and try out effects you haven't explored and see what further variations based on your source image you can generate.

If you only wish to publish and display your artwork digitally, either on a flat video/computer display, or via digital projection onto a screen, as in the case of artwork for the web, for video games, or for film, then at this stage you are ready to reopen your completed artwork in the program of your choice for further processing, editing or integrating into another document.

Coming up in the next chapter is guidance and advice on where to go from here if you wish to print your artwork, how to prepare your painting for printing, some basic printing options and considerations, and some ideas for post-print painting.

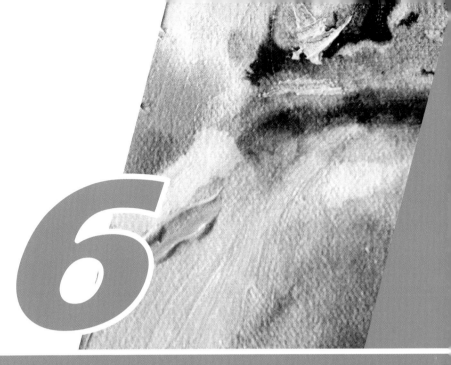

Painting From Photos III— Completion

When is a Painting Finished?

In a chapter on "completion" we need to consider when the painting process is complete. When is a painting finished? There is no one definitive answer to this question. My goal in this chapter is not to give you rules for deciding when your painting is finished and how to finish it, but instead to encourage you to explore taking your painting beyond the computer and into a final physical artwork that you, or your client, will be proud to display.

There are several aspects of completion we need to make decisions on. First there is the completion of the digital paint process within Corel Painter 11. When is the digital painting complete? Beyond the obvious "I have a deadline and whatever state it is in at the deadline is the finish," I recommend that you work on your image until you feel that it is working successfully. Then leave it for a time and come back and take another look. Sometimes taking a step back from your work is needed for you to see it in a fresh light and to see things you missed previously. If you are getting frustrated with your painting, and feel like you are not getting anywhere, that is also a good time to take a break from the image and come back to it later. For this reason I find it valuable to be working on several projects in parallel. That way you can work on one and then take a break from it while you work on another.

When working from photos there is a natural tendency to overwork the image until it almost returns to the original photo. I recommend looking back at some of your earlier versions

Figure 6.1 Framed portrait of Dawn Hampton with post-print paint added.

and putting them side by side with the later versions. Ask yourself which work better as paintings. You may be surprised to find that the earlier, rougher, simpler versions are more effective. You may also find that you wish to bring back selected portions of an earlier stage into a later stage. To do that refer back to the multiple clone source "mix it in" technique described at the end of the last chapter.

The answer to when a painting is finished is also a stylistic choice. I don't feel any of my Painter artworks are finished until they are printed out, usually onto canvas, and have physical paint added. Even then I find myself tweaking and adding to paintings months or even years after I thought they were "finished!"

The bottom line is that you, as the artist, make the call on when your artwork is finished.

Preparation for Printing

The next stage of completion is preparation for printing, assuming the end result you are aiming for is a physical artwork. You have many choices when it comes to printing—whether to print

Figure 6.2 Detail of completed portrait of Dawn Hampton showing post-print acrylic paint on canvas.

in-house or use a service bureau, the type of printing technology to use, what substrate to print onto, how to best prepare your digital file, how to set up your color management system, whether to apply physical media onto your print, how to protect, mount, frame and display your print, and so on. For in-depth discussion of color management and digital printing issues and options, I recommend consulting the many excellent books that are available on the subject, such as *Mastering Digital Printing* by Harald Johnson (Muska & Lipman) and *Practical Color Management: Eddie Tapp on Digital Photography* by Eddie Tapp (O'Reilly). In this chapter I share only what I do in my art studio. This chapter is not intended to be a comprehensive guide to printing and color management. I will leave that to the experts in those fields.

Everything discussed in this chapter could equally be applied to any artwork you create in Painter, whether made with use of photography or not. The only photo-specific instruction is the suggestion to place a small print of your source photo next to your canvas print when you are painting on it.

Choice of Printer and Substrates

In choosing a printer I suggest you start by deciding how large a print you want and on what substrate. Then see if what you want can be printed by your in-house printer. If not you could use an outside service bureau or purchase a suitable printer. Besides the cost factor, one advantage of an in-house printer is the flexibility and convenience it gives you to experiment, proof and print at short notice and with low per print cost (ignoring the initial capital purchase cost) compared with an external service.

Whatever printer you use, ensure that it has durable pigment inks. The current professional imaging large format series of inkjet printers from Canon (ImagePROGRAF Graphic Arts series), Epson (Stylus Pro series) and Hewlett Packard (Designjet series) all use durable inks suitable for long-lasting prints on fine art paper or canvas. My current fine art printers are:

- Epson Stylus Photo 2200, which I use for smaller prints (up to SuperB 13" × 19") on fine art and handmade papers (from www.FlaxArt.com, usually choosing lighter colored ones that do not have a strong pattern or dark features); and the
- Epson Stylus Pro 9600, which I use for wide format prints (up to 44" wide substrates), usually on Water Resistant Matte Canvas (44" × 35" roll from www.DigitalArtSupplies.com), and sometimes on Museo Max fine art paper, also from Digital Art Supplies.

For online one-stop shopping, www.SimplyCanvas.com is a convenient service. They have made test prints for me and I can vouch for their quality. A local service bureau in the San Francisco area that also provides a fine art printing service is www.BlowUpLab.com.

Rough Versus Flat Media

Choosing a print substrate and post-print painting technique that is consistent with the look and feel of your artwork style will lead to a more satisfying result. For instance, when you create an artwork in Painter that you wish to have the look and feel of "rough media," such as oils and acrylics, I recommend printing on canvas (with a surface specially prepared for inkjet printing) and applying physical ("traditional") paint media onto the print. Canvas offers a tough, durable support for working with acrylic or oil paint.

The portrait of Dawn Hampton shown here (Figure 6.1) is one that naturally felt like it needed to be printed on rough canvas rather than a smooth paper. There are many types of canvas available that are specially treated for inkjet printing. They have differing characteristics. If you are doing your own printing I recommend you experiment with samples of different canvases and then settle on the one that works best for your art.

Conversely, when your Painter artwork has the look and feel of "flat media" (Figure 6.3), such as a print (etching, lithograph, woodcut, screen-print or engraving), photograph, watercolor or drawing, then it will be natural to print onto an appropriate substrate such as a fine art or watercolor paper and not apply any paint onto the paper. You may also wish to experiment with handmade papers or non-conventional substrates like bark, papyrus, mylar or metal foils (available from most major art stores such as Dick Blick, Pearls and Flax). If you use a substrate that is not pre-coated for inkjet printing, you may need to treat the substrate surface with an appropriate Digital Ground (see http://www.goldenpaints.com/mixmoremedia/digiground.php) so it accepts inkjet pigment. Not all surfaces will need a digital ground so I recommend you experiment with and without the digital ground, and then decide which works best. You may consider adding crayon, pencil or pastel to prints on paper in a way that matches the style of the flat media and works with the composition.

Figure 6.3 This portrait of the father and daughter dance at Cecilia's quince años, created in the style of a classic French poster print, was better suited to be printed on a fine art paper than on canvas. I worked onto the print subtle pencil and pastel marks. It is framed behind glass, unlike canvas prints, which do not have glass in front of them.

Borders and Edges

Once you have completed your painting in Painter, you will probably find that near the edges of your digital image are wonderful organic brush strokes that are suddenly cut off by a harsh, sharp, straight edge (Figure 6.4).

If you are intending to display your work in a frame where the very edge of your digital print is obscured by the frame, then the harsh straight edge doesn't matter. For example, most traditional mouldings, such as the frame mouldings shown in Figure 6.1, have a quarter inch lip which covers up the outer quarter of an inch of your image all the way round and thus hides the harsh edge.

Figure 6.4 The harsh, straight "computer" edge of the lower right corner of the digital file of the completed Dawn Hampton portrait.

However, if you intend to display your artwork with the edge exposed, for instance a gallery wrapped canvas (Figure 6.5) or a float mounted paper print (Figure 6.6), then the harsh edge will ruin the illusion of the natural media you have used in your digital image. In these cases I recommend you add extra canvas at the border, typically a couple of inches, all the way round and work into the harsh straight edge to make it rougher and more organic in a way that is consistent with the style, colors and textures of the artwork. This will add consistency and authenticity, just as the choice of an appropriate print substrate does.

I add, and work onto, the digital borders and edges after painting rather than before because I find that I can't help but paint to the edge of my canvas, whether I intend to or not. If I added an extra border at the beginning with the intention of leaving it out of the main composition for the purposes, for instance, of wrapping it around a stretcher bar (gallery wrap), I would automatically paint to the very edge and end up losing important elements of the composition in the border.

Another aspect of edges is the edge of the substrate you print onto. If you are printing onto a paper it is a nice touch to have a deckled, distressed edge. Some papers come with deckled edges and some don't. If you tear or cut the paper to a particular size it may end up with a sharp edge. You can artificially deckle and distress the edge of papers with a variety of tools. If you do this I recommend doing so after running the paper through the printer, not before.

Pixel Resolution

Before you add a painted border it is useful to finalize the image pixel resolution for printing. If my file size is smaller than 150 pixels per inch (ppi) I usually resize it up to 150 or 180 pixels

Figure 6.5 The gallery wrapped edge of "Flamenco Jam" (www.jeremysutton.com/flamencojam. html). Notice how the brush marks have been extended into the edge region that wraps around the stretcher bars.

Figure 6.6 "Rick and his Buick Beauty" (www.jeremysutton.com/buick.html) in a float mounted frame where the canvas wrapped around the edge of the stretcher bars is still visible.

per inch prior to printing (in Painter using Canvas > Size with Constrain File Size unchecked, and in Photoshop using Image > Image Size with Resample Image checked). I have printed at many different resolutions and in practice have not found any noticeable difference at pixel resolutions above 150 ppi. This may be a reflection of the impressionist nature of my paintings. I recommend you try some tests for yourself and see if you notice any difference.

Figure 6.7 Select > Select All followed by Edit > Copy.

Please note that the pixel resolution (pixels per inch) of the digital image is a different parameter to the resolution (dots per inch) of the printer, which in turn may be different to the resolution you set in the Printer dialog window. I shall stay focused here on what I do to create my prints and what I have found works best.

How to Add a Painted Border for Printing

There are many different ways to generate a suitable border for printing. Some people flip images at the edges or use special filters and plug-ins, and so on. The technique I share here uses hand brush strokes without any filters, plug-ins or effects. I recommend using a hand brush stroke in place of an automated brush stroke whenever you can since that will always express more of your individuality as an artist.

1   Open your completed painting in Painter.
2   Choose Select > All, or Cmd-A (Mac)/Ctrl-A (PC). Marching ants appear around the image.
3   Choose Edit > Copy (Figure 6.7), or Cmd-C (Mac)/Ctrl-C (PC). If your intention is to print onto paper and float mount the paper in a frame with the edge of the paper showing, then

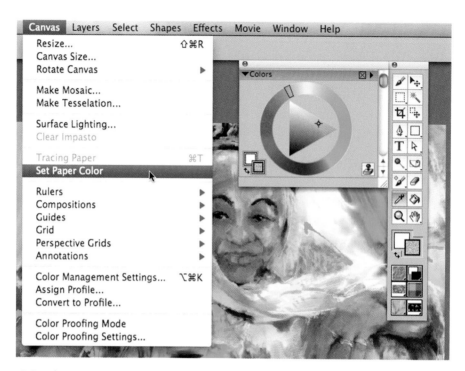

Figure 6.8 Choose Canvas > Set Paper Color to set the paper color for the extra border.

I suggest you skip ahead to step 7 and add extra white canvas to your image. That way your image can merge into the white paper in a natural way. If you are going to print onto canvas then I recommend working with a colored border, in which case proceed to the next step.

4 Choose Select > None, or Cmd-D (Mac)/Ctrl-D (PC). The marching ants will disappear.

5 Click on the "D" key. This chooses the Dropper tool.

6 Click in the final image near an outer edge and pick a color for a border.

7 Choose Canvas > Set Paper Color (Figure 6.8).

8 Choose Canvas > Canvas Size.

9 Add the number of pixels to all sides corresponding to 2 inches. Thus if my file resolution is 100 pixels per inch I would add 200 pixels all the way round (use the Tab key to toggle between each input box). If the resolution were 150 pixels per inch I would add 300 pixels all the way round (Figure 6.9).

10 Hold the Space bar down and click once. This centers the image in the image window.

11 Choose Edit > Paste, or Cmd-V (Mac)/Ctrl-V (PC). This pastes the main image centered over the one with the border added (Figure 6.10).

12 Click on the layer in the Layers list just under the gray triple-layer icon (which signifies a regular image layer) on the right of the layer. This toggles the padlock Lock Layer icon which locks the layer from being accidentally moved, dropped, painted on or altered in any other way.

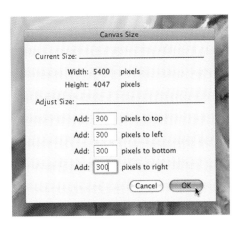

Figure 6.9 Add enough pixels to the Canvas > Canvas Size to ensure 2 inches of extra border to paint into.

Figure 6.10 Choose Edit > Paste and this pastes a copy of the original image as a layer over the background canvas which has the extra border.

13 Choose Shift-Cmd-S/Shift-Ctrl-S (File > Save As).

14 Set the version number to be the next number in sequence.

15 Add "brdr" in the notes section at the end of the file name.

16 Save as a RIFF file.

17 Make the background canvas active (click on Canvas in the Layers palette).

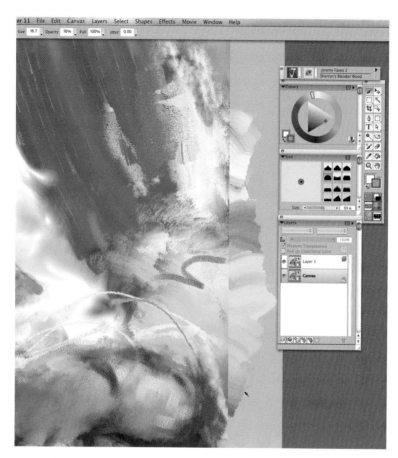

Figure 6.11 Extending brush marks on the background canvas into the extra border. Note that the colors match the colors used in the main image.

18 Choose one of the non-Cloner brushes you used in the paintings which can move a lot of paint. Jeremy Faves 2 > Sherron's Blender Wood, with a little Blenders > Runny, works well for oily style paintings that are going to be printed on canvas. For a watercolor or pastel style painting that is going to be printed on paper, and where you have added a white border, I suggest a combination of brushes such as Jeremy Faves 2 > Artists Palette Knife followed by Tinting > Diffuser2 and Blenders > Grainy Blender 30, and a little Grainy Water 30 at low opacity.

19 Make sure Clone Color is not activated.

20 Use the Option (Mac)/Alt (PC) key to select colors near the border and then drag paint out into the border (Figure 6.11).

21 Work your way around filling the border with paint. You will see a border where the edge of the pasted layer is.

22 Choose Save As and save the next sequential version.

Figure 6.12 Click on Layer Mask icon to generate a layer mask.

23 Choose the pasted layer in the Layers palette so it is highlighted.

24 Click on the Layer Mask icon (right-most of the six small icons at the bottom of the Layers palette). You will see a layer mask appear in the Layers list (Figure 6.12).

25 Choose Chalk > Square Chalk 35.

26 Make the brush size relatively small.

27 Pick black in the Main Color swatch.

28 Gently paint in the layer mask around the edge of the layer in any region where you'd like to fade away the sharp edge (Figure 6.13).

29 Choose Shift-Cmd-S/Shift-Ctrl-S (File > Save As).

30 Set the version number to be the next number in sequence.

31 Add "paintedbrdr" in the notes section at the end of the file name.

32 Save as a RIFF file.

33 Click on the padlock Lock Layer icon. This toggles the lock off. The icon disappears and you can now drop the layer and flatten the image.

Figure 6.13 Paint into the edge of the layer mask using black with a Square Chalk 35, or any other brush of your choice. This fades away the visibility of the edge, showing through what is underneath on the background canvas and softening what is otherwise a harsh and mechanically straight edge. Note that you can still work on a layer mask while a layer is locked since the layer mask doesn't alter any pixels in the layer itself. It only affects their visibility.

34 Choose Layers > Drop All.

35 Choose File > Save As, or Shift-Cmd-S (Mac)/Shift-Ctrl-S (PC).

36 Set the version number to be the next number in sequence.

37 Add "paintedbrdrflat" in the notes section at the end of the file name.

38 Save as a TIFF file. This is the file you will now open in Photoshop for printing.

Color Management

As I mentioned before, this chapter is not intended to give in-depth instruction in color management. However, I just wish to emphasize the importance of regularly calibrating your monitor and creating custom profiles for the printers and substrates you are printing with to ensure the closest correspondence between the colors you see on your screen and those you get out of your printer.

In addition I have found it helpful to set the default RGB profile in Painter (Canvas > Color Management) and the RGB working space in Photoshop (Edit > Color Settings) to be Adobe RGB (1998), and to assign the profile of files to be the same (Canvas > Assign Profile in Painter and Edit > Assign Profile in Photoshop). This minimizes any difference between viewing a file open in Painter versus Photoshop.

Both Painter and Photoshop offer color proofing modes where you can "soft proof" your images on screen. In Painter you would use Canvas > Color Proofing Settings (where you set the device profile) followed by Canvas > Color Proof Mode. In Photoshop you would use View > Proof Setup > Custom and choose the printer profile and media that you wish to use. By choosing Black Point Compensation and Simulate Paper Color, your screen will give you a more accurate rendition of what the print will actually look like. You can then soft proof your file anytime by choosing View > Proof Colors. Add any levels or color corrections with Adjustment Layers so that you do not change the actual pixels of your final image.

I always print out of Photoshop, where I have greater control for printing than in Painter, using the appropriate printer profile and assigning Photoshop, not the printer, to manage the colors. In the Printer dialog window I ensure the color management setting is set to No Color Adjustment. I recommend you talk with your printer and substrate supplier or service bureau, or with a specialized consultant, and get their advice on the best settings and profile for your situation.

Post-Print Painting

Post-print painting, the application of physical paint media and hand brush strokes onto your print, can transform your Painter artwork from a good digital painting into a magnificent work of fine art! Every painting I sell that involves digital painting has physical paint media of some kind applied by hand onto the canvas print. These combined media artworks are one-of-a-kind original paintings, not prints. Aesthetically I am not satisfied with a flat print. Adding physical paint to my prints is an essential part of my creative process and I strongly encourage you to make it part of yours too. The physical brush strokes are what set my paintings apart from looking like reproduction prints. I see my Painter painting process as just part of my complete creative workflow, which includes applying traditional media.

Just as with the pre-print preparation, there are many approaches to post-print painting. The workflow, materials and techniques I share here are simply what I have found work for me in my studio. They are not the "right" way and I encourage you to experiment on every level, with different substrates, different treatments of your prints, and using different types of materials and media.

"Wet" Studio Set Up

Before diving into the nitty gritty of post-print painting, let's first consider what environment we need to prepare for our "wet" studio (as opposed to our digital art studio). I recommend the following:

- Choose a pleasant, well-ventilated, airy room, preferably with large clear (not tinted) windows, high ceilings and good natural light (important when you are painting to be able to see what your colors really look like in daylight). If you are going to paint by artificial light, choose daylight standard lighting (such as certain halogen bulbs) and avoid regular incandescent bulbs or the dreaded fluorescent tubes.
- As much clear table-top space as you can make available, preferably at least two 3' × 6' surfaces at a comfortable height to work on and ideally on wheels so they can be easily moved. Have enough space to lay down your artwork flat on one surface and arrange your paints and other materials on the other surface.
- Cover both surfaces with "butcher" paper taped down.
- On the surface where you will place your paints and tools I recommend completely covering that surface with white freezer paper, shiny side up.
- Place protective drop cloth on the floor below the tables, and wear painting clothes and a protective apron, to protect from flying paint!
- Dedicate a wall space that you can get dirty for pinning up your painting. Remember to place a drop cloth on the floor below the wall.
- Have plenty of thick kitchen towels available, plus small jars of water for washing brushes and a water sprayer for keeping acrylic paints moist.
- You will also need large quantities of masking tape, freezer paper and cling film.

Fixing

When a print emerges from my printer I usually leave it to "breathe" for a few hours before taping the unstretched canvas vertically on a wall and spraying it with a fixative such as PremierArt Printshield (Figure 6.14), a lacquer based spray designed specifically for all inkjet prints (see www.inkjetart.com). Golden also offers a range of inkjet spray fixatives that include UV protection (see www.goldenpaints.com/mixmoremedia).

I spray on three coats, alternately spraying vertically and horizontally across the print for each coating, in a well-ventilated environment (preferably outdoors) and using a protective mask. Always fix your print before applying any other media. If you are trying out a technique for the first time try it on a proof print rather than risk ruining your final print.

Gelling

After fixing the print and before applying any paint, I lay the print down on a flat horizontal surface and apply a transparent acrylic gel over the entire surface of the print. The transparent gel

Figure 6.14 PremierArt Printshield spray fixative.

adds texture and also serves as a base onto which to add acrylic paints and other physical media. Applying the gel before paint is the opposite of the way that transparent varnish is historically applied as a finishing layer at the very end, after all the paint has been applied. The terms "gel," "medium" and "varnish" are used somewhat interchangeably. In general a gel has a thicker viscosity than a medium or varnish. All of these are essentially colorless paint. Colored paint is typically made of colored pigment or particles suspended in a medium.

For the transparent gel layer I usually use Utrecht Gloss Acrylic Medium & Varnish (Figure 6.15; see www.Utrecht.com.) I apply it fairly liberally with a flat brush, size 12 (Figure 6.16), in brisk, energetic brush strokes that correspond to the forms and movement in the painting, extending the brush strokes beyond the edge of the printed area.

I moisten the brush first in water and then hand-dry it with a paper towel. This helps keep the brush in good condition. Golden also offers a variety of acrylic gels and mediums that you

Figure 6.15 Moist flat brush being dipped into a jar of Utrecht Gloss Acrylic Medium & Varnish. Notice the bucket of water and the blue paper towel—both useful to have available during this stage of the process.

Figure 6.16 Applying gel onto the canvas with a flat brush size 12. Notice the amount of gel loaded on the brush and that it appears milky white. It will dry transparent.

may wish to try out. For detailed descriptions and comparisons (see http://www.goldenpaints.com/products/medsadds/gels/gelreview.php.) I recommend using a gloss gel since they dry the most transparent. You always have the option in finishing to apply a matte medium or varnish if you wish to suppress the gloss sheen.

Acrylic gels usually look milky white when first applied, and then they dry transparent, provided they are not applied too thickly. After covering the whole canvas with brush strokes I double-check for "bald" patches, that is, areas that I have accidentally missed. Since the gel is glossy and the ungelled substrate is matte, by looking at a suitable oblique angle it is easy to spot the bald patches.

After completing the gelling make sure you thoroughly clean your brush in warm water with a washing up liquid. Acrylic is basically plastic glue and will ruin your brush if you allow it to dry hard on the bristles.

Painting

Choosing Your Paint

For ease of use, non-toxicity, speed of drying and convenience I recommend regular Golden acrylics. These are high quality paints that, like all regular acrylics, dry very quickly, sometimes within minutes if applied thinly. Of course, quick drying can be both a benefit and disadvantage. You have to take care to use the paints you lay out on your palette quickly or cover them up to prevent them drying before you have a chance to use them.

At the other end of the spectrum are traditional oil paints, which in general offer a wider, more luscious range of colors than acrylics, which stay malleable, mixable, blendable and "wet" much longer than traditional acrylics (thickly applied oil paint may take months or even years to dry all the way through!). The thinning and cleaning agents associated with using traditional oils include toxic and carcinogenic products.

Between these two extremes is a growing range of modified acrylic and oil paints that bridge the gap between the two worlds. On the oil side there are now faster drying water-soluble oil paints that eliminate the need for toxic solvents and behave more like acrylics—for example the Winsor and Newton Artisan Water Mixable Oil paints (see www.winsornewton.com/products/oil-colours/artisan-water-mixable-oil-colour/).

On the acrylic side is the new range of Golden Open Acrylics (see www.goldenpaints.com/products/color/open/index.php) that stay malleable much longer than regular acrylics, and behave more like traditional oil paints. Ironically, when you are used to the convenience of having your painting ready to go within hours of applying regular acrylics, it can take some adjustment to get used to the much longer drying times of the new Open acrylics. The advantage, of course, is that you can keep blending the colors on your canvas for longer and your palette doesn't dry up so quickly.

I suggest starting with the regular acrylics, which the remainder of this chapter focuses on, and then experimenting with the other options according to your level of interest and curiosity. If you are really interested in broadening your knowledge of acrylic paint and getting more creative ideas of what you can do with it, I recommend the book *Rethinking Acrylics: Radical Solutions for Exploiting the World's Most Versatile Medium* by Patti Brady (North Light Books, 2008).

Choosing Your Colors

Unlike in Painter, where we are spoilt with 24 million potential colors easily accessible at our fingertips (especially with the new expandable Colors and Mixer palettes), in physical paint we need to prepare by purchasing the colors we wish to work with ahead of time and then use those colors to make all the other colors we may wish to use.

An easy option is to purchase a pre-made regular acrylic starter set, such as the GOLDEN Principal 8 Color Mixing System which includes: Hansa Yellow Medium, Naphthol Red Light, Quinacridone Magenta, Phthalo Blue (GS), Phthalo Green (BS), Yellow Ochre, Zinc White, Titanium White and a Color Mixing Guide. These are all Heavy Body colors which I like since this allows you to build up nice impasto (thick) brush strokes on your print. Heavy Body colors are well suited for use with a palette knife.

In my experience the addition of more colors to choose and mix from will broaden and enrich the range of colors you end up applying in your painting. I purchase my acrylic color in jars, a selection of which are shown in Figure 6.17, rather than tubes. Jars usually contain more paint and prove more economical if you are using large quantities. I work with approximately 40 different colors, chosen with the assistance of Peggy Gyulai and based on her oil colors palette. For this reason I describe this selection of colors, and the way I arrange them on my palette, as "Peggy's palette." Please note that economics can also play a role in your choice and quantities of colors, with some colors and brands being much more expensive than others. The cost of 40 large jars of acrylic paint can easily add up to many hundreds of dollars. I suggest you start with small quantities and see which colors you use up first. Golden is an excellent brand which I recommend for high quality acrylic paint.

Figure 6.17 Majority of Peggy's palette by jars.

Laying Out Your Palette

There are literally thousands and thousands of alternative ways you can lay out your colors on a palette, and many different types of palettes to choose from. Here I am referring to the non-digital meaning of the word "palette," that is, the physical surface you distribute your colors onto for blending and for loading onto a brush, palette knife or other tool used for depositing the paint onto the canvas surface. More important than the particular system you use to lay out your colors is simply to have a consistent system that you stick to. A consistent palette system allows you to quickly, efficiently and repeatedly set up your palette and get painting.

My physical palette surface is my flat, horizontal table surface covered in the freezer paper. I only place relatively small amounts of each color onto my palette. This minimizes waste, especially since regular acrylics dry so quickly. I use a broad flat palette knife (Figure 6.18) to transfer paint from my jars of paint onto my palette surface, wiping the knife clean with a cloth between colors to prevent accidental cross-mixing of colors. To prevent the jars being sealed closed by dried acrylic (which acts like a glue once dry), I coat the seal of each jar with vaseline before closing it up. I also paint a sample swatch of the color contained in each jar on the lid for ease of recognizing which jar is which.

To keep my regular acrylics wet I regularly spray them with water and, if leaving them for some time, cover them with kitchen cling film. There are also many other alternatives, such as custom-made palette dishes with airtight lids or placing petri dishes upside down onto the paint blobs.

I arrange my colors (Figures 6.18 and 6.19) grouped by hues from left to right: whites, yellows, earths/browns, orange/reds, violet/blues, teal/greens, and gray/black. There are variations of the hues in each column. The most important colors are along the top two rows.

Figure 6.18 Using a broad flat palette knife to transfer paint from a jar to the palette. Note the small dab of paint. Be wary of putting out too much paint, at least initially until you can more accurately judge how much you think you'll need.

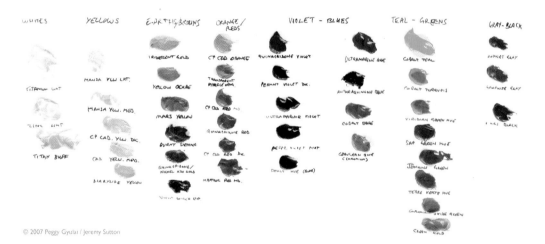

© 2007 Peggy Gyulai / Jeremy Sutton

Figure 6.19 Peggy's palette by blobs on freezer paper.

Mount Your Print and a Small Source Photo

Mount your still unstretched gelled print onto a vertical surface like a wall or board on an easel. I like to use a wall and either use push pins or staples to secure the canvas. Also mount a small (6" × 9" is sufficient) print of your source photo, on the upper left of your main gelled print, to refer to as a visual reference. Place your palette table adjacent to your painting so you can easily look back and forth between the palette and the painting as you choose and mix colors.

Applying Paint

My primary tool for applying acrylic paint onto my prints is a long narrow palette knife with a raised handle (Figure 6.20). I like the sculptural way that a palette knife can deposit and

163

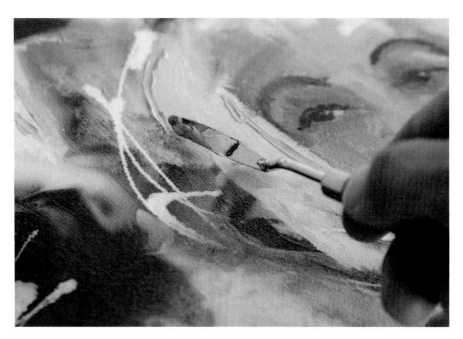

Figure 6.20 Applying paint onto the canvas with a thin palette knife. Notice the amount of paint piled onto the knife and also the way it contains streams of different colors not quite blended together.

manipulate paint on the canvas. A brush will tend to produce a subtler, smoother, more blended effect, which may be appropriate for some parts of the painting. The choice between palette knife and brush, or any other paint application tool for that matter, is purely a stylistic one and is an artistic decision that only you can make. If you are new to painting with physical paint I suggest you experiment with both palette knives and brushes. Work on an artist's proof print that you don't mind ruining and just go for it! Just like in Painter, we need to become familiar and comfortable with our tools before we can control and master them.

The key question with applying physical paint onto a digital print is what colors to apply where. Since you already have a completed digital painting, the goal is not to cover up lots of your wonderful digital brushwork with acrylic paint. Instead I suggest you look at where accents of color could enhance and enliven the composition and bring out contrasts or focal points.

My approach is to not over mix and blend colors, but instead to create rough juxtapositions and partial blends on the mixing region of my palette, that is, an area clear of the color swatches. I then load these unblended colors onto my palette knife. I first make a practice move-ment with the loaded palette knife over the canvas in the air and then make the actual brush stroke, starting in the air and making a single, sometimes quite slow, sweeping motion, twisting the palette knife and exhaling as I go, and continuing to extend my motion even after the palette knife is no longer in contact with the canvas. I leave the paint thick, as it came off the palette knife. I avoid, wherever possible, going back over the brush stroke and "smushing" the paint down, flattening and spreading it onto the canvas and over the digital printed image. It is tough avoiding the temptation of "smushing" but well worth it!

I usually start with experimental strokes in the edges of the image where it is less critical and then, as I get warmed up, start working along lines of contrast in the composition where contrasting blocks of tone and color meet (Figure 6.21). I work into both highlight and shadow areas as it feels appropriate to do so.

Once I have loaded my palette knife with color I move it around in front of the painting, looking for areas where I may be able to use that paint. I frequently work on more than one painting simultaneously and look for places in all the paintings where I can use particular colors. If I have color left over on the palette knife I continue to search for places I can use it in.

This process continues until I feel there are no more places on the painting I wish to add paint to. I will then typically leave the painting up for a few days and revisit it a few more times to see if anything draws me to add more paint, or to add any finishing layer of varnish. I generally like the finish of the dried acrylic and do not add varnish. There have been situations where a client places a painting of mine in a location that catches the sun at a glancing angle at certain times of the day, leading to too much reflection. In that case I have applied a matte varnish over the painting surface.

Once all the painting is complete and the acrylic has had a chance to dry (regular acrylics will be dry within hours, depending on the ambient temperature and humidity), I remove the painting from the wall. The painting is now ready for stretching, if it is on canvas, and framing.

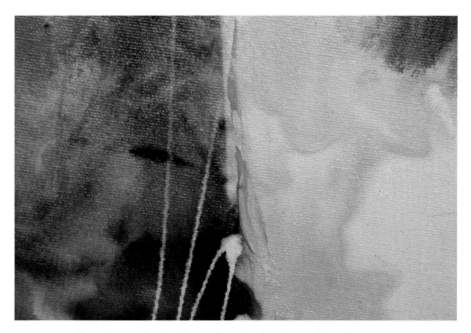

Figure 6.21 Acrylic paint applied with a palette knife along a line of contrast. Note that I don't worry about getting it exactly aligned.

Conclusion

I encourage you to take your digital paintings to the next level with the application of traditional physical media onto your prints. The end results will be more interesting and, as I mentioned earlier, they will also be unique, one-of-a-kind combined media artworks.

I have endeavored to share in words in this chapter what is best seen in live action. To learn more effectively about my painting techniques I recommend joining PaintboxJ.com, where you will be able to see these processes demonstrated on video, and attending one of my classes. I teach a workshop titled "Traditional with Digital" which is devoted to learning about combined traditional-digital painting techniques, including post-print painting.

As much as adding physical paint accents to your digital prints enhances your finished painting, it is not enough without a strong underlying image, composition and effective use of color and tone, whether you are painting from a source photograph or from direct observation of a subject. One of the biggest challenges in working from photos, besides the attachment to detail, is getting away from the photo color. In the next chapter—, "Going for it with Color!"—we look at ways to work with, and expand your range of, color.

7

Going for it with Color!

The notes are right underneath your fingers, and all you gotta do is take time out to find the right note. That's what life is, we all got notes underneath our fingers and we gotta take time to find the right notes, to come up with our own music.

This advice, that the late great musical legend Ray Charles (Figure 7.1) gave Jamie Foxx in preparing for the film *Ray*, applies equally to colors as to musical notes. In expressing ourselves through our art we naturally come up with our own colors…

The exercises in this chapter are designed to help you make confident, bold color decisions, and realize the full power of color in expressing yourself and your impression of your subjects. Whilst many of the exercises start with working from a photo reference, you can apply exactly the same techniques and exercises to working from direct observation. This chapter builds on what you have already learnt earlier in Chapter 3 on how to choose color using the Colors, Color Variability, Mixer and Color Sets palettes. Before we dive into color exercises I'd like to first review some color basics.

About Color

Color is a Perception

Sir Isaac Newton (Figure 7.2), the seventeenth century scientist and mathematician who made some of the most profound discoveries about the nature of light, wrote: "To determine… by what

Figure 7.1 Portrait of Ray Charles.

modes or actions Light produceth in our minds the Phantasms of Colours is not so easie." Color is not a physical entity like light. Color is a perception.

The color we perceive when we focus our gaze on a specific region in our visual field reflects how our brain processes information about the wavelength, intensity and luminance (value) of light from that region as well as the influence of the light from surrounding regions.

Hue, Saturation and Value

Artists generally describe colors by three characteristics: hue, saturation and value. Hue is the named color (red, orange, yellow, green, blue, indigo, violet, and so on) independent of saturation or value. Saturation is brightness/dullness or intensity of hue. The extremes of saturation are 100% hue at the most saturated, and value only, independent of hue (that is, grayscale: black, white and grays) at the most desaturated. Value is luminance or lightness/darkness or tone. The extremes of value are pure black and pure white.

There is no absolute pure black or white in what we see around us in everyday life. One of the ways that the French Impressionists broke away from the historical emphasis on lights and darks (*chiasco charo*) was to eliminate black from their palettes and use whites blended with other

Figure 7.2 Phantasms of Colours—Portrait of Sir Isaac Newton, 2007, 24 inches × 30 inches.

colors. If you look at a white or black object or surface depicted in, for instance, a portrait by John Singer Sargent or an impressionist scene by Pierre-Auguste Renoir (Figure 7.3), then you'll see many colors used even in the lightest and darkest areas of the paintings. Make a point to carefully observe original paintings up close and see the range of colors used and the way the brush strokes have been applied (Figures 7.3–7.6).

In the remainder of this chapter I will use the terms "value," "luminance" and "tone" interchangeably. Within Painter you will also find all three terms used:

- "Value" in Saturation/Value Triangle and the HSV color info;
- "Luminance" in the Using: Image Luminance or Original Luminance options in many of the Effects menus;
- "Tone" in Effects > Tonal Control.

Figure 7.3 Observing the *Luncheon of the Boating Party* (1880–81) by Pierre-Auguste Renoir, on display at the Phillips Collection, Washington D.C.

Primary Colors

Because most of us have three types of cones (color sensitive cells in our eyes), three suitably chosen primaries (primary colors) can generate all other colors. Because our cones have broad absorption ranges (and therefore respond to a broad range of wavelengths of light) we are not too particular about which colors are primaries. Margaret Livingstone (*Vision and Art: The Biology of* Seeing, Abrams, 2002)

Thus the phenomenon of there being three primary colors from which all other colors can be made is a result of our biology. Exactly what those primaries are is not set in stone. Red, yellow and blue are typically primaries in connection with paint pigment, and red, green and blue are typically primaries in connection with light. The use of primaries in a painting can help create a dramatic, strong mood. An example of this is *Brother Ray* (Figure 7.1), where red, green, blue and yellow are all dominant colors in the composition.

Figure 7.4 Detail from Renoir's *Luncheon of the Boating Party*. Notice the variety of color in the man's white shirt, which includes reflections of blue from the environment around him. The dark band around his hat, which looks plain black at first sight, is full of subtle hues on closer inspection.

Color Wheel

A traditional artist's color wheel is an arrangement of colors designed to help artists choose, combine and mix paint colors effectively. It is typically created by initially placing dabs of the three primary paint colors—red, yellow, and blue—equidistant around a circle. Adjacent primary colors

Figure 7.5 Detail from Renoir's *Luncheon of the Boating Party* showing a white tablecloth and white napkin that are not so white after all! Renoir's dark areas are just as full of colors as his light areas.

are then mixed to create secondary colors (for instance, yellow and blue are mixed to create green). Dabs of the secondary colors are placed halfway between the primary colors from which they are made. This process is continued with tertiary colors made up by mixing primary colors with secondary colors around the wheel, and so on until there is a continuous range of colors around the wheel.

Summer Afternoon (Figure 7.8) is a painting dominated by colors that lay between the primaries on the color wheel, such as cyans, teals, magentas and oranges.

Painter's Hue Ring (Figure 7.9) is an approximation to a traditional artist's color wheel, albeit with the physics primary colors of red, green and blue being equidistant around the wheel instead of the traditional red, yellow and blue paint primaries. The secondary colors on the Painter Hue Ring are cyan, magenta, and yellow, the colors associated with C, M and Y in CMYK printing.

As you may gather from this description, Painter's Hue Ring is not exactly the same as a traditional artist's color wheel but can serve a similar purpose. Rather than get caught up in color theory, I suggest you simply make use of the Hue Ring by choosing colors you like and

Figure 7.6 There is so much to see in this detail from Renoir's *Luncheon of the Boating Party*. The darkest blacks are in fact deep blue. The whites are warm creams mixed in with many other colors. Besides demonstrating Renoir's diversity of color in his darks and lights, this detail also shows the vigor and variety of his brush strokes. You can almost feel the bristles of Renoir's brush as you see the dynamic yellow strokes across the brim of the hat.

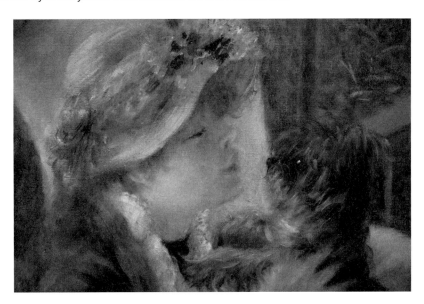

Figure 7.7 By comparing this desaturated (grayscale mode) version of Figure 7.6 with the full color version you can see what a difference hue makes. For instance the orange flowers on the hat can hardly be seen in the grayscale and yet sing with vibrance in the color version. In grayscale the hat brim and shirt ruffles have similar prominence; in color the yellow jumps forward. The yellow-red scarf is almost indistinguishable from the dark jacket in grayscale and yet is more striking in color.

Figure 7.8 *Summer Afternoon* (http://jeremysutton.com/summerafternoon.html)—notice the dominant colors: cyans, teals, magentas and oranges.

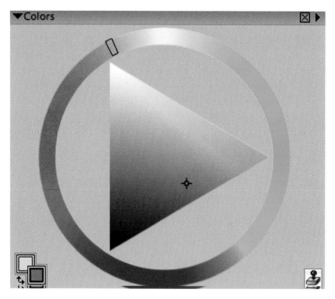

Figure 7.9 Hue Ring—Corel Painter 11's equivalent of the artist's color wheel. Note that when you drag the Colors palette out from the group of palettes so it is unattached to any other palette, you can then expand it by dragging on the bottom right corner of the palette. The expanded Colors palette gives you much more precision for determining the hue in the Hue Ring and the saturation and value in the Saturation/Value Triangle.

juxtaposing colors connected by simple geometric relationships. Here are a few suggestions for choosing colors to juxtapose next to one another in your painting:

- Two colors that are on opposite sides of the Hue Ring (complementary colors);
- Colors from the warm red-orange-yellow side versus colors from the cooler blue-green side;
- Three colors that are equidistant around the Hue Ring (thirds or triads);
- Three tertiary hues that are equidistant from each other on the color wheel, such as red-violet, yellow-orange and blue-green (tertiary triads, see Figure 7.12);
- Colors from a limited band of adjacent colors on the Hue Ring (analogous colors); or
- Accenting analogous colors with a complementary color from the across the Hue Ring (split complementary).

Complementary Colors

As referred to above, two colors are complementary when they are exactly opposite each other on the color wheel. When complementary colors are blended together in traditional paint they neutralize each other to produce gray. When pure, unblended complementary colors are juxtaposed adjacent to each other in a painting, they can have a powerful effect on one another, bringing out a vividness in each other. As painters we can take advantage of the fact that our eyes naturally seek to balance any given color by its complementary color. When the complementary color is not present, the eye spontaneously generates the complement. We can use combinations of complementary colors in a work to provide harmonious balance, as well as bring attention to specific areas of the image. See the use of complementary colors to emphasize a point of interest in *Island* (Figures 7.10 and 7.11).

My approach to color is not to over analyze or theorize but to follow my intuition and trust my eyes. Remember you're in the driver's seat and, irrespective of theories and schemes, you have the freedom to combine any colors you want!

The Dependence of Colors on One Another

Although one can determine the hue and brightness of a color physically by wavelength and luminance, there is no such objective constancy to the perceptual experience. Depending on its neighbors, a color undergoes startling changes in appearance. In a painting by Matisse the deep purple of a robe may owe much of its saturated redness to a green wall or skirt bordering on it, whereas in another area of the painting the same robe loses much of its redness to a pink pillow or even looks quite bluish in response to a bright yellow corner. Depending on what local association one is looking at, one sees a different color.

Rudolf Arnheim (*New Essays on the Psychology of Art*, University of California Press, Berkeley, 1986)

As Arnheim so eloquently explains, the underlying issue in perceiving color is color relationships. Every color is influenced by every other color around it. You can use this phenomenon,

Figure 7.10 *Island* 2006, 40 inches × 40 inches. This painting, shows modern dancer Tiffany Barbarash moving in the Yerba Buena Gardens, San Francisco (part of the Cityshapes series, an artistic collaboration between Tiffany and myself).

known as the "color surround effect," to your benefit when applying color in a painting. A touch of color here and there can affect the whole mood and feel of the painting.

You can see an example of color surround effect in my live portrait of Jan Di Nuoscio (Figure 7.13) where a single brush stroke of a secondary color, magenta, in the lower right corner changed the color dynamics of the whole portrait, which is largely primary reds, yellows and blues.

Perceived Saturation & Tone

Colors have inherent perceived saturation and tone. For instance, green has an inherently brighter perceived saturation and lighter perceived tonal value than red. The inherent value of a color is independent of the value adjustments you may make in Painter's Saturation/Value Triangle. Sometimes a colorful painting will look vibrant and full of life and seems to powerfully describe the lights and darks in a scene, and yet when we desaturate the image, using, for instance, the

Figure 7.11 Notice the use of two complementary colors, orange and bright blue, juxtaposed close to Tiffany's face, the main point of interest in the painting.

Underpainting palette's Saturation slider (Figure 7.14), the image seems flat and lacking in strong light-dark contrasts. What we can take away from this is simply to trust our perception of what works and doesn't work in a painting when it comes to using color.

Value Study—Black and White Thumbnail

The practice of looking for and depicting relative tonal contrasts will help you in using color effectively. It will also free you up to use colors other than what is in your source photo, without losing the integrity of the image. In this exercise you will create a rough value study of your subject, starting by blocking out the main areas of lights and darks and then refining the study to include more graduations of value. Your visual reference will be a color and a desaturated version of your source image. The color version allows you to see perceived tone that is influenced by the colors in your image. The desaturated version makes it easier to see the lights and darks

Figure 7.12 *The First Dance—Portrait of Annette and Roman*, 2006, 24 inches × 36 inches. Notice the Tertiary Triads in the accent strokes on Annette's dress.

without getting distracted by color. The main purpose of this exercise is to practice careful observation, not what the study ends up looking like.

1 Click on the Tab key to hide palettes.
2 Place your source on the upper left of your Painter desktop.

Figure 7.13 *Jan Di Nuoscio*, 2006, 30 inches × 34 inches. Note the effect of the magenta brush stroke in the lower right corner.

3 Zoom out using the Magnifier slider at the bottom of the image window and make your image thumbnail size.

4 Choose Canvas > Rotate > 180. This turns your image upside down. It is useful to make a "180" shortcut button in a custom palette if you don't already have one.

5 Choose File > Clone to make a clone copy.

6 Choose Window > Underpainting so the Underpainting palette is visible (no need to do this if it is already visible).

7 Take the Saturation slider in the Underpainting palette all the way to the left.

8 Click Apply in the Underpainting palette.

9 Close the Underpainting palette.

10 Choose Save As and save this version using the P-V-N naming system.

11 Choose Cmd-Shift-E (Mac)/Ctrl-Shift-E (PC) to apply the Effects > Tonal Control > Equalize effect.

Figure 7.14 Notice how the desaturated version of the portrait of Dawn Hampton loses the distinction between the bright teal accent strokes and the yellow. In the desaturated version these two colors have very similar tonal value, yet their perceived tonal value indicates the teal is lighter than the yellow. The bright red is also perceived as distinctly darker than the adjacent yellow and yet can hardly be differentiated from the yellow in the desaturated version.

12 Click OK.

13 Choose Save As.

14 Zoom out on this grayscale version of your image and place it below the color version on the left of your Painter desktop.

15 Choose File > Clone to make a clone copy of the grayscale version.

16 Click on the Tab key to show palettes.

17 Choose a slightly darker than mid-gray main color in the Saturation/Value Triangle, with cursor all the way against the left side of the triangle. Whenever your cursor is all the way on the left side of the Saturation/Value Triangle the resulting grayscale color is independent of wherever the cursor is on the Hue Ring.

18 Choose Edit > Fill or Cmd-F (Mac)/Ctrl-F (PC) with the Fill With: Current Color radio button selected in the Fill dialog window. This fills the clone copy with the gray you just selected in the Colors palette. At this point you may find that your window background color, which by default is a mid-gray, is so similar to your gray canvas that it's difficult to discern the background again. In that case return to the Saturation/Value Triangle, choose a dark gray (move the cursor lower down the left side of the triangle), choose Corel Painter 11 > Preferences > Palettes and UI (Mac)/Edit > Preferences > Palettes and UI (PC), and click Window Background: Use Current Color.

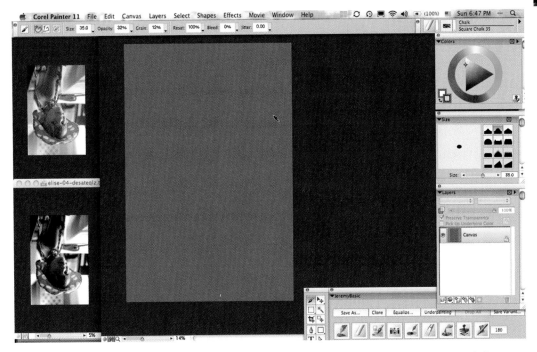

Figure 7.15 A "small-small-BIG" layout in preparation for a tonal study for a portrait of Elise.

19 Choose Save As.

20 Make your gray canvas large on the right side of your desktop (Figure 7.15) to make a "small-small-BIG" arrangement.

21 Choose Chalk > Square Chalk 35 in the Brush Selector palette. This choice of brush is not critical. You could easily do this exercise with many different brushes.

22 Make the chalk relatively large compared to your canvas size.

23 Half close your eyes and look at the lights and darks in your image.

24 In a few quick big brush strokes map out the main rough blocks of light and dark with your chalk in the gray image.

25 Look for the very lightest and very darkest shapes in your image.

26 Now reduce the size of the chalk a little and depict these shapes. Don't worry about getting the positioning and scale exact. This exercise is all about seeing value. Do not use Clone Color or Tracing Paper.

27 Continue this process, gradually working into more refinement and differentiation between contrasting shapes of different values. As you get into refining the study, you can gradually use limited cloning (using the desaturated version as clone source) to help get the positioning and scale more accurate. Keep it loose and don't worry too much about details.

28 Every now and then step back and half close your eyes to compare the lights and darks in all three images. Then continue to work in your tonal study until you are satisfied you have

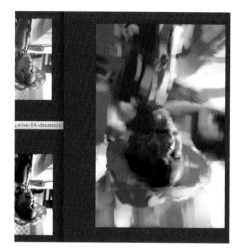

Figure 7.16 The tonal study. Note that it is not a detailed or exact painting but simply a rough study.

described the main tonal relationships in your composition and can clearly see the lightest lights and darkest darks (Figure 7.16). Make sure to use Save As regularly and keep up the sequential version numbers.

29 You can test whether your tonal study has successfully encompassed the full range of tone by choosing Cmd-Shift-E (Mac)/Ctrl-Shift-E (PC) to apply the Effects > Tonal Control > Equalize effect. If the Equalize effect makes a big difference then you know you were painting within a narrow range of grays and not depicting the darkest darks and lightest lights. Either way, after applying the Equalize effect, choose Edit > Undo or Cmd-Z (Mac)/Ctrl-Z (PC) to undo the effect. If Equalize didn't make any noticeable difference then you are finished; if it made a noticeable difference work into your lightest lights with a very light value and darkest darks with a very dark value until you find Equalize makes no difference.

30 Choose File > Save As and include "tonal study" in the notes at the end of the P-V-N file name.

Mid-Tone Color Study—Expressing Tone Through Color

In the previous exercise you depicted relative values using only the grayscale, independent of hue. In this exercise you will depict relative values using only mid-tone colors, that is, colors from the mid-tone (halfway up) section of the Saturation/Value Triangle. As with the tonal study, the value of this exercise is learning to see relative values and then describe them on your canvas. It is not about producing a perfect likeness of your subject so please don't worry if your proportions or positioning are off.

1 Zoom out of the tonal study you just completed so it is the same thumbnail size as the color and desaturated source image versions.

2 Place the zoomed out tonal study on the lower left of your Painter desktop.

3   Click on the color version of your source image so it is the active image in Painter.

4   Choose File > Clone.

5   Choose the Dropper tool (keyboard shortcut "D").

6   Pick a mid-tone color from within the image.

7   Choose Effects > Fill or Cmd-F (Mac)/Ctrl-F (PC).

8   Make sure Fill With is set to Current Color.

9   Choose OK. The canvas fills with current color.

10   Choose File > Save As.

11   Make this clone copy large on the right side of your Painter desktop in a "small-small-small-BIG" arrangement (Figure 7.17).

12   Limit yourself to using non-clone colors whose value is restricted to the central horizontal band across the middle of the Saturation/Value Triangle, that is, the mid-tone tonal range. The colors can be any hue, not just the colors you see in your source image. Thus you cannot depict lights or darks by pulling the Saturation/Value Triangle cursor into the white or black corners. Your only color variables are hue and saturation. Using just these two color variables, and any brushes (in Figure 7.18 I used the Artists > Sargent Brush), create a painting based on your photograph. Look back and forth regularly between your large working image on the right and the three thumbnail images on the left to determine whether your brush stroke color needs to be adjusted to describe the tonal relationships in your composition. This is not an easy exercise! You will need to experiment with different colors to find those that work

Figure 7.17 The "small-small-small-BIG" arrangement.

Figure 7.18 An early stage of a mid-tone color study.

Figure 7.19 The mid-tone color study in progress, depicting tonal contrasts by varying the hue and saturation, rather than the value, of the brush stroke colors.

best in communicating the right relative value in each part of your composition. As with the Tonal Study exercise, work with the images all upside down. This helps you disconnect from being concerned about what you are painting and instead focus on accurately observing the source as an abstract pattern of shapes of differing value and contrasts.

13 Spend at least an hour developing your painting with this color restriction. You can rotate all the images by 180 degrees so they are the right way up (Figure 7.19).

14 Choose Save As. Save your image into your project folder using the P-V-N naming convention.

Wild Color!

This exercise is about letting go of rules and restrictions. The colors you choose need not bear any relationship or resemblance to the actual colors you see. It's as if you've been giving some special multicolored glasses which expand your color horizon and permit you to see a vastly increased range of colors in the world. Be free from worry about what color should be where. Trust that you will find them.

Allow your self to step outside the lines and improvise (Figure 7.20). Be bold, be daring, be crazy, be wild! Play with different combinations of colors next to each other. Test out the effect of

Figure 7.20 Portrait of musician and composer Marcus Shelby.

juxtaposing complementary colors from opposite sides of the color wheel. Paint in a way that you may not have dared to before. Use whatever brushes you like. This is an exercise where you are being given permission to step out from being safe. Your canvas is a laboratory for experimentation. Make the most of it and enjoy!

Mixing Variations Together

By the time you have completed the exercises described thus far in this chapter, you will have generated a number of alternative versions of your image. If you wish to further extend your creative explorations then you could mix in from all of the variations into a final image. To do this, follow the "mix it in" technique described near the end of Chapter 5.

Emulate Different Artists' Styles

As a final color exercise you are going to tread in the footsteps of other artists. There is a long tradition in the history of art of copying other artists to learn about their use of color, brush stroke, value and technique. This is always a valuable exercise for stretching your own use of color and trying out ideas you may not naturally have tried. You will always learn something, even when you don't like the result.

1 Choose three different artists who have distinct artistic styles and ways of using color. Ideally visit museums and galleries and see the artists' works in person. Otherwise consult books that have good reproductions of artwork.

2 First choose one painting from each artist. Using Painter and visual reference only, without using any cloning, Clone Color or Tracing Paper, paint copies of the three paintings. For example I chose to create a copy of Henri Mattise's *Femme au Chapeau* (Figure 7.21).

3 Then create three original paintings based on your own photographs or from observation or imagination, each of which emulates the style of one of the three artists. I created a painting (Figure 7.22) of my mother, Margaret, based on the style Matisse used in *Femme au Chapeau*. When doing this exercise you may find it useful to use a custom color set based on the colors of your chosen artist. I have included several color sets based on famous artists' paintings on the Resource Disc with this book. You can also easily make your own by scanning or photographing paintings, opening the digital image in Painter and then using the New Color Set from Image command in the Color Set pop-up menu.

Practice, Practice and More Practice!

In this and the previous three chapters I have shared an overall creative workflow with lots of options, choices, exercises and techniques to try out along the way. To make the most of this instruction, and to hone your skills both technically and artistically, I recommend you follow the workflow and techniques with different source images and subjects. The old adage "practice,

Figure 7.21 Copy of Henri Mattise's *Femme au Chapeau*.

practice and more practice" is certainly applicable in this case. The more you try these ideas out the more they will become second nature.

In Chapter 5 I listed three challenges with painting from photos, the second of which was: "Too Easy to Stick with Photo Color." I hope that the exercises in this chapter help you overcome this challenge. Every challenge is also an opportunity. Expanding your range and variety of colors beyond the colors present in your source photograph will make a huge difference to your painting. I like a painting to look and feel like a painting rather than a photograph. If someone looks at one of my paintings and asks "is that a painting or a photograph?" then I know I haven't gone far enough with my brush work and color. A painting like *Summer Afternoon* (Figure 7.8) is clearly a painting and no one has ever asked if it was a photograph or a painting.

Figure 7.22 Mum—in the style of Matisse.

If you are a professional portrait photographer and you are concerned about your clients not liking your colorful artistic interpretations, make two versions: one conservative "safe" version that you think your client will like, and one "just for yourself" version where you have fun and allow the painting to develop in a more adventurous direction. Show your client both versions and give them the choice. I suspect they will go for the "just for yourself" version much more than the more conservative version. Track the decisions over a year and then send me an email with the result (which I'll report in my next book!). One student who did this found that in almost every case her clients selected the one she did for herself.

One aspect of digital painting we haven't covered yet is the art of collage portraiture, the topic of the next chapter. This is an exciting direction for you to experiment with that builds on everything else we have covered so far.

8

Collage Portraiture—The Art of Combining Multiple Images into a Portrait

Introduction

This chapter describes my approach to combining multiple images into what I call a "collage portrait." There are many terms for combining multiple images in an artwork, such as "collage," "montage," "combines" and "assemblages." What you, or others, label your artwork, style or technique is less important than what you say with it and the impact it has. My concept of a collage portrait is an artwork that reads as a portrait and combines many visual elements that relate to the portrait subject. Thus a collage portrait is not a pure collage or a pure portrait painting but a combination of both.

In this chapter you will learn the primary techniques and methodology I used in creating collage portraits such as the two examples shown here: *Skycap Keith* (Figure 8.1), which is also featured on the cover of this book, and *San Francisco Heart* (Figure 8.2). More examples of my collage portraits are featured in the following "Gallery" chapter. The principles, strategies, workflow and techniques shared here, and also shown on PaintboxJ.com, can be applied to creating a collage portrait of any subject such as one or more persons, a family, a business, an animal, a vacation or trip, a place, a building, an event or a city. I use the term "portrait" in the widest sense of the word. My goal in sharing the creative path that led to this artwork is to inspire and empower you to create your own personal collage portraits.

Figure 8.1 *Skycap Keith*, 38 inches × 57 inches, pigment and acrylic on canvas, 2009 (www.jeremysutton.com/skycapkeith.html).

Figure 8.2 *San Francisco Heart*, 40 inches × 60 inches, pigment and acrylic on canvas, 2009 (www.jeremysutton.com/sanfranciscoheart.html).

My collage portrait workflow varies with every portrait I paint. Sometimes I create a complete photographic collage and then transform it into a painting, as in the case of *San Francisco Heart*. Other times I transform my foundation image into a painting first and then add collage elements, as in *Skycap Keith*. There are no rules. Don't restrict yourself by following strict formulae or recipes. Instead master the techniques and apply them as they feel appropriate. The order and way you apply techniques will differ from project to project. The most important aspect of your collage portrait is not your choice of media or techniques—it is what you say in your art, what you express about your subject, the story behind the painting and the passion you share.

What is a Collage Portrait?

When I use the term "collage portrait" I am referring to a painted portrait of a subject in which there is usually one main foundation image interwoven with a multitude of subsidiary images, some more subtle than others, but all contributing to the whole in a harmonious and meaningful way. A collage portrait is distinct from a photo-collage, a montage or an array of juxtaposed images where no image dominates. It is also distinct from portraits made up of thousands of micro-images that act like pixels, becoming an invisible part of the fabric of the final image and only discernible upon close inspection.

In the collage portraiture we discuss in this chapter, each subsidiary image, larger and smaller, is a symbol of something significant in the life of the portrait subject. The artwork can tell a story about the subject that bridges space and time. Space is bridged across the canvas geographically with the places shown and time is bridged through use of historical photographs and documentation, bringing the past into context with the present.

Background

Skycap Keith depicts a skycap named Keith who kindly helped Peggy and I with our bags when we arrived at the Phoenix Sky Harbor airport on our way to Imaging USA 2009. Ironically it was because one of our bags missed the flight (Figure 8.3) that I met, and had time to photograph, Keith and obtain his permission to use his picture as a demonstration case study in my Imaging USA keynote presentation and, subsequently, in this book. If you look carefully you'll find the Delayed Baggage Receipt subtly featured in the background of the painting between Keith's right shoulder and the "Skycap" lettering. After starting the painting during my presentation I continued working on the image at my booth in the trade show and thereafter back in my studio, starting with mainly brushwork, transforming the foundation image into a painted portrait, and then applying many elements as paper textures. Then, after printing it out on canvas, I applied acrylic paint.

San Francisco Heart was inspired by my experience of living in San Francisco and wanting to express my appreciation of the beauty, diversity, creativity, excitement and richness of this beautiful "City by the Bay." In preparing for this collage project I went on photo shoots around the city at different times of the day and night, and, in addition, drew upon thousands of photographs I have taken over the last 10 years. From all these images I selected a few favorite images that

Figure 8.3 My delayed luggage unintentionally led to the painting *Skycap Keith* being created. The Delayed Baggage Receipt shown here symbolizes how a seemingly adverse setback can be turned into a plus, just like my approach to laying down brush strokes in a painting…

formed the basis for this collage. I picked out a foundation image (the Golden Gate Bridge, which serves as an internationally recognized symbol of the city) and selected a few other favorite images that I felt would be good for use as subsidiary images. I copied and pasted the secondary images onto the foundation image and worked with a combination of layers, free transforms, layer masks, cloning, paper textures and brushes to complete the artwork. It was printed out on canvas and I worked onto the print with acrylic paint, gold leaf and chin collé.

The workflow that I followed with both these examples, and that serves as my general approach for making collage portraits, consists of five distinct stages:

I   Research
II Select and Sort
III Define Template Size
IV Digital Techniques
V   Post-Print Techniques.

The remainder of this chapter examines each of these stages in turn.

Stage I: Research—Acquire Source Images

My collage portraits can take anywhere from days to years to create from start to finish. Six months to a year is the estimate I give my clients. Initially there is an idea, an inspiration, a vision. The initial spark is followed by an intense period of research during which you allow your idea to gestate as you seek out and acquire imagery. I recommend you take your time with the research stage. My research stage may take months. The power and beauty of your final artwork reflects the diversity of your source material and the depth of your understanding of your subject.

Copyright

Collage by its very nature encourages the use of found images: cuttings from magazines, images from the internet, and so on. Many such found images are copyrighted, even if they do not include a copyright notice, and making small changes or using the image as a basis for a hand-painted derivative image may still be a copyright infringement. Ideally I recommend using your own photographs whenever possible and always getting a signed model release. Respect other people's copyright, just as you would expect them to respect yours.

When making use of other sources of imagery seek to identify and contact the copyright holder and request permission for usage. Document and record all your sources of imagery and give attributes and acknowledge photo credits in any usage. There are many resources that can help you with copyright issues. Here are a few:

- www.copyright.gov/help/faq
- www.graphicartistsguild.org/resources/ask-mark
- www.calawyersforthearts.org/legalservices.html

If you are a member of a professional organization, such as the Professional Photographers of America, American Society of Photographers or the Graphic Artists Guild, they often offer legal advocacy and consultation services, including copyright advice, to their members. If you are in any doubt, and especially if you intend to exhibit, publish, enter in a contest or sell your image, I recommend consulting a legal professional.

In the research stage I take the time to listen to my subject and find out from them what is most important in their life, their passions, hobbies, people and places they love. I seek their input on what they would like to see represented in the painting. Sometimes they prepare a list and bring specific photos and documents to show me. Rather than keep any valuable family heirlooms and irreplaceable photographs, I simply use my camera like a scanner and photograph their photographs. When capturing photographs taken by others seek permission from the subject and, if possible, the original photographer, for usage of the image as a component in a collage. Request for such permission is built into my standard Art Agreement that I have every client sign prior to commencing on a portrait commission.

I intensely observe and obsessively document! I look out for details, for textures, writings, photos, scenes as well as shots of my subject (Figure 8.4). At every meeting I have my Canon 5D with a Canon EF 24–105 mm f/4 L IS USM lens, with extra batteries and CF cards at the ready. I love working with my 5D since it is light but tough, captures large enough files for painting from, but not too large, and is a full-frame digital single lens reflex (SLR) camera so I can capture more for a given aperture than with non full-frame SLRs. The lens is a fantastically versatile general purpose lens that is great for close up detail shots, mid-range portraits, wide-angle environmentals and zooming in from afar.

Figure 8.4   Photographing Keith at the airport.

In the case of Keith I ended up taking 52 source photographs in 30 minutes, averaging almost two shots a minute. I captured them in RAW small JPG. RAW gives me the most leeway and flexibility, especially important since I use natural light and often purposely underexpose to capture movement in low light conditions. In low light situations I set my camera to 3200 ASA (H setting). For painting purposes I am not bothered by the grain that results from using such a high ASA setting. In this example there was plenty of light.

Stage II: Select and Sort—Choose Primary and Secondary Images

Organize Your Project Folder System

Having a good project folder structure and organization is absolutely essential for any collage project you undertake. Every file must have its unique home on your computer or your external storage device. This allows you to always easily and quickly locate your files and in turn frees you up to be more creative. I recommend that you first make a dedicated project folder for each collage project. Name it in a meaningful way so you know immediately what is in the folder. Save it in an appropriate place on your computer. Remember you may be coming back to this project many times over many months, or even years. I name my project folders with the year–month of commencing the project and the project name (e.g., "09.01 Skycap Keith") and save it in a project section of my hard drive. I find the two-digit year–month useful at the beginning of my project folder names since then all my projects line up chronologically when listed in my Finder browser.

Once you have completed the research phase of your project and acquired your source images, the next step is to determine if and how you will use them in your collage composition. I use iViewMedia Pro or Aperture to preview and sort through my source images, and save the favorites as flat RGB TIFF files. There are many alternative browsing and cataloging programs available that you can use for this task. I look for a single main foundation image and multiple secondary images. The foundation image acts like a compositional anchor for the artwork, setting the main structure and framework onto which many other layers of imagery can be added. The secondary images support the main composition and will be smaller and more subtly woven into the artwork than the foundation image. I call candidates for the foundation image "primary images." I use the term "candidates" meaning that your choices at this stage are not set in stone. You can always add more images later, and you can always choose not to use an image selected as either a primary or secondary candidate.

Before sorting through your source images and selecting primary and secondary images, first create an organized sub-folder system within the project folder to save them into. I suggest using the following sub-folder names, each beginning with a shortened project name of seven characters or less:

- Custom Data
- Original Photos
- Primary Images
- Secondary Images
- Working Images.

These five sub-folders will line up in this order when listed in your computer. Use the same consistent shortened project name throughout, at the beginning of all these sub-folder names as well as at the beginning of all your working image names (using the Project-Version-Notes, P-V-N, file naming system). Below is a summary of what each sub-folder is for:

- The Custom Data sub-folder is where you may save custom paper libraries, and other custom Painter data, created specially for this project.
- The Original Photos sub-folder is where you would save a copy of the original photo files that came out of your camera, including all the RAW files, from all the photo shoots you make for this project. This is an optional sub-folder that ensures that you will always be able to conveniently access all the information associated with a project at any time in the future.
- The Primary Images sub-folder is where you will save candidates for the foundation image.
- The Secondary Images sub-folder is where you will save candidates for secondary images.
- The Working Images sub-folder is where you will save all the versions of your working files as you document the development of your project.

Choose Your Foundation Image

Once you have reviewed all your source images and saved your favorites into the primary and secondary folders, revisit your primary images and pick the one that you feel stands out as the best to serve as an anchor for your collage. It may be that there is only one stand out foundation image in which case you may not need a Primary Images sub-folder. Whichever image you choose as your foundation image (Figure 8.5 for *Skycap Keith* and Figure 8.6 for *San Francisco Heart*), that image forms the first version in your Working Images sub-folder.

Figure 8.5 This is the photo selected to be the foundation image for *Skycap Keith*. When making a portrait I always seek out a foundation image that conveys the personality of my subject and that has good eye details. This image succeeded in conveying the subject's personality, included good eye detail and also provided plenty of space in the background to work into.

Once you have selected your foundation image save it, using the P-V-N naming system, into your working images sub-folder as version 01. Then apply the same steps to this version 01 as are described in Chapter 4 for enhancing your photograph and refining the composition.

Identify Dominant Secondary Images

Look through your secondary images. See if there are any that stand out as being more dominant than the others. For instance, in the case of *San Francisco Heart* one such dominant secondary image was the golden heart sculpture (Figure 8.7), created when local artists were invited to paint large hearts that were placed around the city and then auctioned off to raise funds for charity. I pictured weaving this heart into the Golden Gate Bridge.

We will use this heart later in this chapter as an example to illustrate how to introduce a portion of one photo into another. The other secondary images selected for *San Francisco Heart* (Figure 8.8) reflect my personal experience and view of the city. They included landmarks and vistas like the city skyline (seen from Treasure Island), the City Hall, the AT&T Ballpark Coca Cola sculpture, the Mission Dolores, the Gates of China Town, the Palace of Fine Arts, the new de Young Museum tower, the SFMOMA roof, the Japan Town tower, the Transamerica Pyramid and the Twin Peaks antenna, as well as symbolic icons such as a trolley car, a cable car, the "One Tree" sign, the SF Giants logo, Nob Hill Café, the KFOG fireworks, fishing boats at Fisherman's Wharf, the North Beach "Condor" neon sign and a map of the city. These images were captured in RAW and opened using the Adobe Photoshop CameraRaw window.

Figure 8.6 For *San Francisco Heart* I settled on this photograph of the Golden Gate Bridge as my foundation image. The bridge is the ultimate icon of San Francisco and this particular image allows lots of space around the bridge to play with in the collage.

Figure 8.7 Photograph of the golden heart in the garden of one of my clients. I chose this to be a major secondary image for *San Francisco Heart*.

Figure 8.8 Browsing through some of the secondary images for *San Francisco Heart*.

Figure 8.9 This close up of Keith's hat was chosen to be one of the secondary images that I knew I wanted to use in the collage as a paper texture. I will use Keith's skycap symbol to illustrate the paper texture collage technique later in this chapter.

The secondary images for *Skycap Keith* included visual elements, such as the details on Keith's hat (Figure 8.9), that I could picture adding as textures in the painting, though not as major photo collage elements in the same way that the heart would become such a central component of *San Francisco Heart*.

Stage III: Define Template Size

Once the source images have been chosen and saved into the appropriate folder, the next task is to define a consistent template size for use throughout the project. Sticking to a consistent size for all your working files and clone sources is the key that simplifies everything. Without a consistent template system you will find yourself getting very confused when you try to clone from multiple source images that are all of different sizes and resolutions.

1 Open your foundation image in Corel Painter 11 and choose Canvas > Resize (Figure 8.10).

2 If your width and height units are in pixels, change them to inches.

3 Uncheck Constrain File Size.

4 Adjust the image size to match the desired end result. Please refer to the section titled "What Resolution?" for discussion on size and resolution.

5 Click OK.

6 Choose Save As and save the image with the next version number.

As with your source photos for painting, choose Effects > Tonal Control > Equalize, or Cmd-E (Mac)/Ctrl-E (PC), followed by Window > Underpainting > Photo Enhance > Saturate to enhance the image for painting. Increase the tonal contrast and saturation of painting source images beyond where you would go if you just wished to make a photographic print.

Choose File > Save As, or Cmd-Shift-S (Mac)/Ctrl-Shift-S (PC), and name your resized foundation image template with the following P-V-N naming convention: short project name–two-digit version number–width × height at resolution, all rounded to the nearest whole digit; for instance "keith-03-57 × 38at77.tif." Since this is a flat image with no brush strokes it's okay to save it as a TIFF file.

In general, save all your working collage files as Painter RIFF files (the native format of Painter) to preserve all data and maximize the future editability of the file in Painter, especially important in collage work because of all the layers you will be creating.

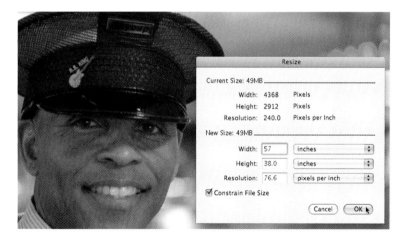

Figure 8.10 Resizing the skycap foundation image to set the template size, I decided to leave the number of pixels constant; hence Constrain File Size is checked, and I set the inches to be what I was aiming for. I then stuck with this exact size for the remainder of the creative process in Painter. I normally print from a file at 150 pixels per inch (ppi) but chose to work at a lower resolution to keep my file sizes down.

Choose File > Clone and resave the clone copy as a Painter RIFF file with the next version number and a note saying "workingimage," for instance "keith-04-workingimage.rif." This will now be your working image. From now on the notes section of your P-V-N file names can be used for a short description of what this version contains, what effect was applied or which brush was used. Adopt the same small-BIG arrangement described in Chapter 5.

Stage IV: Digital Techniques—Different Ways to Mix and Blend Imagery

There are two principal ways that I digitally mix and blend one image into another in my collage portraits—one is a copy & paste layer technique and the other is a paper texture technique. Each technique has a number of variations in the details of how you apply it, but the principal techniques boil down to those two choices.

These techniques are in addition to the painting techniques already discussed in Chapters 4 through 6. My collage portraits usually have one of two painting workflows—one where I first construct a photo collage which I then use as a basis for painting, the other where I first paint the foundation image and then add more elements after that, painting each as needed. The paper texture technique I usually apply near the end of the collage construction process.

Technique #1
Copy & Paste Layer Technique

The easiest way to introduce a portion of a secondary image into the working image is as follows:

1 Open the secondary image in Painter.
2 Select the portion of the secondary image you wish to paste into your working image. There are many ways to make selections in Painter and you can use any of these to select portions of your image. If you wish to simply select the whole image you would choose Select > All, or Cmd-A (Mac)/Ctrl-A (PC). I find that I tend to use the Freehand Selection tool and make a quick, rough selection around the area of the image I am interested in. I then choose Select > Feather and feather the freehand selection by about 30 pixels (Figure 8.11).
3 Choose Edit > Copy, or Cmd-C (Mac)/Ctrl-C (PC).
4 Now make the working image the active image in Painter.
5 Choose Edit > Paste, or Cmd-V (Mac)/Ctrl-V (PC).
6 You will now see the selected portion of the secondary image pasted over the working image as an image layer listed in the Layers palette.
7 Double click on the Image Layer name in the Layers palette.

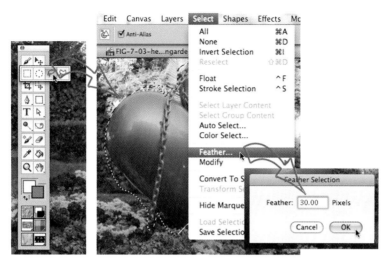

Figure 8.11 Feathering a freehand selection.

8 Rename the layer in the Layer Attributes dialog window to describe what the layer is.

9 You can move the position of the layer using the Layer Adjuster tool on the top right of the Toolbox. This tool is automatically selected when you paste into an image.

10 One useful "trick" is to purposely lower the layer opacity (using the slider in the Layers list) so you can visually reference what is underneath the layer. When you have it positioned, scaled and oriented as you wish you can then put the layer opacity back up to 100%.

Resize and Rotate by Converting to Reference Layer

You may wish to change the scale and orientation of the layer you introduce. The most flexible way to do this is as follows:

1 Select the layer in the Layers palette, making sure that it is not locked (that the Locked Layer icon does not appear next to the layer name).

2 Choose Layers > Convert to Reference Layer (Figure 8.12). This has changed from earlier versions of Painter, when it used to be Effects > Orientation > Free Transform. In Painter 11 there is a Photoshop style free transform listed under the Edit menu but it does not have the flexibility of the reference layer to remain editable across saves. The reference layer has faintly visible control handles (small squares) in the corners and halfway along the sides. If the layer is larger than the background canvas the control handles may be situated beyond the edge of the image. You may need to put your image in Screen mode, or Cmd-M (Mac)/Ctrl-M (PC), and zoom out, Cmd-"-" (Mac)/Ctrl-"-" (PC), to see the handles.

3 Hold the Shift key down while dragging in a corner control handle to resize the layer, keeping the aspect ratio the same.

Figure 8.12 Choosing Layers > Convert to Reference Layer.

4 Hold the Cmd key (Mac) or Ctrl key (PC) down while dragging in a corner handle to rotate the layer.

By default the Layers palette only lets you see four layers in the Layers list at one time. If you have more than four layers and wish to see them in the Layers palette all at once, hold the tip of your cursor down on the last row of pixels along the bottom of the Layers list and then drag down. This expands the Layers palette and allows me to view all my layers at once (Figure 8.13). You can click and drag layers up or down in the Layers palette to determine their order. The background canvas, labelled "Canvas", is always at the bottom of the Layers list and can not be dragged from that bottom position.

Control Layer Visibility with Layer Masks

Layer masks allow you to create a finely controlled and smoothly blended visual transition between the edge of a layer and what lies underneath.

1 Make active the layer you wish to work with. You can do this either by clicking on the layer with the Layer Adjuster tool (top right of Toolbox), provided Auto Select Layer is checked (left of Property Bar), or by clicking on the layer in the Layers palette.

2 Click on the small solid black triangle in the top right corner of the Layers palette. This accesses the Layers palette pop-up menu.

3 Choose Convert To Default Layer in the Layers palette pop-up menu (Figure 8.14). This returns the layer from being a reference layer to being an image layer, which you can paint on and control the visibility of through use of a layer mask.

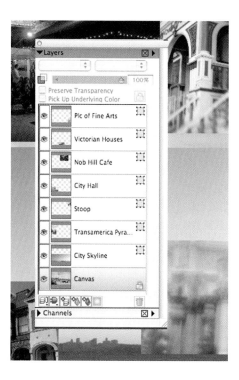

Figure 8.13 Multiple reference layers listed in an expanded Layers palette.

4 Click on the Create Layer Mask icon (Figure 8.15)—the right-most icon in the row of six icons at the bottom of the Layers palette. You will see a black square against a white background appear immediately to the right of the layer thumbnail in the Layers list.

5 In the Brush Selector choose Airbrush category > Digital Airbrush variant.

6 In the Color palette take the Saturation/Value Triangle cursor to the bottom left corner to select pure black as your Main Color (front square). If the Additional Color (back square) is not white then use the Color Swap icon (small curve with arrow on either end situated between the Main and Additional Color squares in the lower left of the Color palette) to swap round the Main and Additional Colors, select pure white, then click once again on the Color Swap icon to make black your Main Color.

7 Make sure that the layer mask is active (it will be bold in the Layers list) and then paint black onto the visible part of the layer in your image (Figure 8.16). Where you paint with black in the layer mask you will see the image in the layer disappear. If instead you see black appear on the layer undo the brush stroke and reselect the layer mask. It is likely that you were inadvertently painting black on the image layer instead of the layer mask. If you want to bring back any of the layer image visibility just click on the Color Swap icon to make white your Main Color and paint with white in your layer mask. White in the layer mask makes the image in the layer reappear. Remember, as in working with Photoshop layer masks, black reveals what is underneath the layer and white conceals what is underneath.

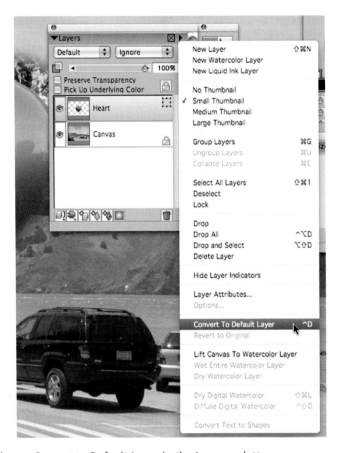

Figure 8.14   Choose Convert to Default Layer in the Layers palette pop-up menu.

Group, Collapse and Lock Layers

The Layers palette allows you to organize and control your layers. This is especially important when you build up multiple layers in a single working image. You will see all your layers listed in the main central part of the Layers palette. I refer to this list as the Layers list. You can group layers together by holding down the Shift key as you select them (by clicking on them) in the Layers list and then select Layers > Group (also available from the pop-up menu accessed by clicking on the icon on the left at the bottom of the Layers palette). While the Group is closed in the Layers list you can only select or move the layers as a group. If you open the Group in the Layers list you can select and move individual layers. By selecting a closed group and then choosing Layers > Collapse, you can collapse a group of layers into a single layer.

Once you have made adjustments to a layer and you wish to preserve those adjustments and avoid accidentally moving or changing the layer, it is a good idea to lock the layer (or group of layers). You do this by selecting the layer in the Layers list and clicking once on the right-hand end

Figure 8.15 Click on the Create Layer Mask icon in the Layers palette.

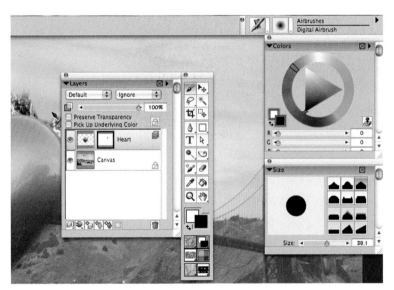

Figure 8.16 Paint into the layer mask with black Digital Airbrush to reveal what is beneath the layer.

of the layer beneath the layer type symbol (Figure 8.17). Clicking in this location toggles the Locked Layer icon on and off. As mentioned earlier the bottom layer in the Layers list is not really a layer at all but is in fact the background canvas of your image. This bottom "layer" is always called "Canvas" and is always locked—you cannot change its name or unlock it.

Figure 8.17 Clicking on the lower right side of a layer in the Layers list toggles the lock on and off. This example shows the *Reynolds and Brown* collage portrait at an early photo assemblage stage. Note that almost all the layers have been named by double clicking on the layer title, are reference layers for maximum flexibility, and are locked to ensure they stay in the right location. You can see the finished result in the following "Gallery" chapter.

Experiment with Composite Methods and Layer Opacity

Composite methods (accessed through the pop-up menu in the upper left of the Layers palette) control the way colors in a layer are affected by colors beneath the layer. They are the equivalent of layer blending modes in Photoshop, though there are some composite methods like Gel, Magic Combine and Pseudocolor that are unique to Painter and that do not have a corresponding blending mode in Photoshop; likewise there are Photoshop blending modes like Vivid Light, Linear Light, Pin Light and Hard Mix that don't have corresponding composite methods in Painter. Experiment with the composite methods. I find Gel, Overlay, Hard Light and Multiply often give interesting results and are a great way to introduce imagery and textures into a composition.

Sometimes I lower the layer opacity for a more subtle effect (Figure 8.18). To change the opacity of an entire layer, first select that layer in the Layers palette and then adjust the Layer Opacity slider (situated above the Layers list).

Make a Clone Source Template

One powerful way to work with copy and pasted secondary images is to make the working files that contain the secondary image layer into clone sources. In this approach you would follow the same instructions as above to create what, in effect, is a clone source template. Instead of just continuing to work on that same working image, you would instead reopen an earlier version (prior to when the layer was pasted in) which becomes your current working image, set the clone

Figure 8.18 In this stage of the *Reynolds and Brown* portrait you can see the Ivy layer with Overlay composite method and the layer opacity lowered to 41%. Note that all other layers have been dropped (flattened) by this point. I only keep layers for as long as I feel I need the flexibility to make changes in them. I drop (flatten) them as soon as I can. Flattening layers reduces the size of your file, which increases the speed of all operations you do to that file.

source template version as clone source (Figure 8.19), and paint it into the working image with the Soft Cloner, or any other clone brush.

The advantage of using a clone source template is that you know your secondary image is positioned and scaled exactly right. You can also, for maximum flexibility, clone into a transparent layer. This clone source template approach is more complex than just adding a secondary image to the working image as a pasted layer. You can also work with multiple clone source templates and alternate between them. As long as all the clone source template files have exactly the same size and resolution as your working image you don't need to worry about the particular size and resolution of your secondary image source files.

Periodically Flatten and Paint

When working with multiple layers I recommend you periodically choose Layers > Drop All to drop all your layers and flatten your working image. Before flattening your working image always save a version as a RIFF file. You will need to unlock any locked layers before you are able to use the Drop All command. If you subsequently have more secondary images you wish to introduce, start building up a new set of layers. This strategy of periodically flattening your working image keeps your file sizes manageable and ensures you are always able to conveniently see all your layers at once in the Layers palette. Flattening your image also has the benefit of allowing you to use brushes to paint over, blend, smear and distort your imagery on a single, flat background canvas.

Figure 8.19 The clone source template, seen here in the lower left of this screen capture, is manually set to be clone source using the File > Clone Source menu. This clone source template was used only to soften the subjects' faces in the upper right of the working image. You can see illustrated here the value of short project names at the beginning of your P-V-N (Project-Version-Notes) file names. If the project names are too long you will not be able to see the file version numbers in the Clone Source menu and tell which file is which.

Technique #2
Custom Paper Texture Technique

Capturing a secondary image, or portion of a secondary image, as a custom paper texture allows you to introduce it into your painting using a grainy brush and any colors you choose. The end result can have a graphic screen-print feel. The technique lends itself to a subtle and versatile way to blend imagery together. The secondary imagery you blend in using this technique can be photos, musical scores, logos, motifs, handwriting, and so on. I developed this technique when I first discovered the versatility of Painter's paper textures back in the early 1990s, and have used it ever since in most of my digital collages.

Skycap Keith includes various motifs, logos and symbols from Keith's cap and sweater that were introduced into the painting with use of custom paper textures. In making *San Francisco Heart* I captured and applied custom paper textures of the San Francisco map, of the Giants logo, and lettering from the Mission Dolores entrance.

There are two distinct approaches to applying the custom paper texture technique. In one approach you just save a custom paper texture that is a different size, usually much smaller, than your working image, and then apply it in a repeating pattern. Any paper texture will automatically repeat, or tile, ad infinitum. In the other approach you create a paper texture template that is exactly the same size as your working image, or exactly 25% of the size (see later for a more in-depth explanation of this option), and have the texture fit the working image instead of repeating. This latter approach gives you more control over where, and at what scale, your texture appears in your image. Before explaining these two approaches to applying the custom paper texture technique, let us first discuss exactly what is meant by paper texture in Painter.

Painter Paper Texture 101

In Painter you'll find the words "paper," "texture" and "grain" used interchangeably throughout the program. In this primer I shall explain what is meant by these words in Painter. Paper texture in Painter is, of course, not real paper texture but an illusion that works very well in emulating the way that grainy dry media, such as chalks, charcoal, crayon, and so on, are affected by different paper textures. Paper texture in Painter is actually a repeating grayscale rectangular or square tile that acts as a filter for certain grainy brushes (brushes that have the word "Grainy" in their method subcategory, viewable by choosing Windows > Brush Controls > General > Subcategory) and can also be applied as a filter on most effects (applied by selecting Paper under the Using menu within the Effects dialog window).

Since the paper texture is actually a filter and not a property of the canvas, it can be changed at any moment without retroactively affecting anything already on the canvas. This gives you a lot of versatility in applying paper textures to your image. You can experience this versatility by choosing any grainy brush and using it with different paper textures. Grainy brushes are distributed throughout the brush categories, and are usually accompanied by a Grain slider being visible in the Brush Property Bar. There are certain brush categories for which every brush in that category is a grainy brush. These "grainy" categories are: Chalks, Charcoals, Colored Pencils, Conte, Crayons, Felt Pens, Oil Pastels, Pastels and Pencils. To change paper texture you can either use the Paper Selector pop-up menu in the Toolbox palette (it is at the top left of the six selectors at the bottom of the Toolbox palette), or by opening the Windows > Library Palettes > Papers palette. I prefer the latter option, opening the Papers palette, where you have a better preview of the paper grain and much more control. Take a moment to experiment with different grainy brushes and paper textures.

The grayscale paper texture tiles act like topographic maps that represent the three-dimensional relief of a rough surface. The 256 levels of gray (from black to white) in the paper texture tile represent the highest points of the surface with the darkest levels of gray, and lowest points with the lightest levels. Black represents the mountain tops and white the valley bottoms. As you drag a piece of chalk over a rough surface the pigment particles typically get deposited on

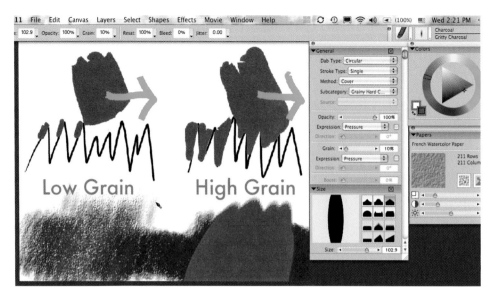

Figure 8.20 The higher the Grain value the less clearly you see the grain defined since the valleys fill with pigment.

the mountain tops but not in the valley bottoms. So it is with the Painter paper textures. Grainy brushes deposit color into the dark areas of the grain and leave the lighter areas untouched.

As you press harder with a chalk the pigment gets deposited progressively deeper into the valleys of the rough surface until it reaches the valley bottoms and you no longer see the relief topography reflected in the chalk marks. This is the same in Painter, except that it is the Grain slider that controls how deep the pigment penetrates into the valleys. The higher the Grain slider value, the deeper the penetration and the less you see the texture (Figure 8.20). This is a little anti-intuitive since at first you may assume that a bigger grain value means more visible grain, but it is in fact the opposite way round. By the time the Grain value is 30% and above, most grainy brushes appear to paint a solid brush stroke without the paper texture being visible at all. I find that the optimum Grain value is often lower than the factory default. For instance, with the Chalk > Square Chalk 35, I lower the Grain value from the default of 12% to about 9%. At a Grain value of 0% it is as if you have lifted your chalk away from the surface altogether, and you will see no pigment deposited. Try varying the Grain value and see this for yourself.

There are two powerful ways you can manipulate the paper texture in the Papers palette. One is to click on the Invert Paper icon—this is the right-hand one of the two icons and shows two arrows going in opposite directions. The Invert Paper icon inverts the darks and lights in the paper grain so what was black becomes white, and so on. This allows you to paint into the so-called "negative" space of your original paper grain. The second powerful feature is the ability to change the scale of the paper grain anywhere from 25% to 400%, which introduces varying scales of paper into your painting.

Repeating Custom Paper Texture

1   Open the secondary image you wish to capture, or a portion of which you wish to capture, as a paper texture.

2   If it is only a portion of the secondary image you wish to capture as a paper texture, then choose the Crop tool (third tool down on the left of the Toolbox), drag it over the region you wish to capture, and click in the cropped area.

3   To make an effective paper texture it is best to capture it from a high contrast black and white image. If your texture source image is lacking in strong dark and light contrast you can use the Equalize effect, Shift-Cmd-E (Mac)/Shift-Cmd-E (PC), to increase contrast, or, better still, choose Effects > Surface Control > Express Texture for a more effective way to create a good texture.

4   Experiment with the Express Texture sliders until you get a high contrast image that preserves details (Figure 8.21). As you adjust the settings look at the effect in the preview window. This will help you hone in on the best values for your image. The exact optimum slider settings in the Express Texture dialog window will vary for every image.

5   Choose File > Save As and save your black and white version of your texture source image.

6   Choose Select > All, or Cmd-A (Mac)/Ctrl-A (PC).

7   If you do not have the Papers palette showing on your Painter desktop, then choose Window > Library Palettes > Papers. You will then see the Papers palette appear.

8   Click on the small solid black triangle in the top right corner of the Papers palette. This accesses the Papers palette pop-up menu.

9   Choose Capture Paper (Figure 8.22), the first item in the Papers palette pop-up menu (not to be confused with the similarly named Make Paper which is the second item in the menu).

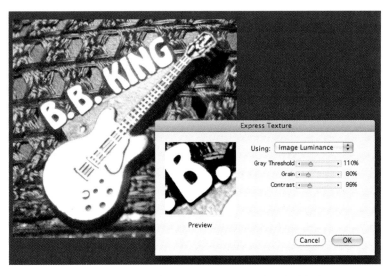

Figure 8.21   Using the Express Texture effect to exaggerate the dark/light contrast in a secondary image—in this case Skycap Keith's B. B. King pin—in preparation for creating a strong paper texture.

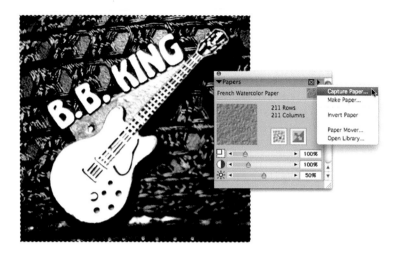

Figure 8.22 Make a Select All and then choose Capture Paper from the Papers palette pop-up menu.

10 Name the custom paper.

11 Set the Crossfade slider to 0. This slider determines how much each repeating tile of texture fades into the adjacent tiles.

12 Click OK. You will now see it appear in the Papers palette preview window.

13 You can now close the texture source image. You will be asked if you wish to save changes on closing since you made a Select All. There is no need to save changes.

14 Choose the Chalk > Square Chalk 35.

15 Lower the Grain from the default 12% to about 9%.

16 Choose a dark color.

17 Create a new layer in your working image by clicking on the New Layer icon (third from left in the row of icons at the bottom of the Layers palette), or Shift-Cmd-N (Mac)/Shift-Ctrl-N (PC).

18 Paint the texture into the image. Change colors as you paint it in. Notice how the paper texture repeats.

19 Try clicking on the Invert Paper icon (right-hand icon in the Layers palette) and painting in the negative space of the paper texture with a lighter color (Figure 8.23).

Custom Paper Texture from a Template

To ensure that your custom paper texture is scaled, oriented and positioned precisely I recommend capturing custom papers from a template of exactly the same dimensions as your working image. This approach is more complex than the repeating texture approach described above but offers greater control.

1 With the current working image active, choose File > Clone. This makes a flat clone copy of the working image. This clone copy will become the paper texture template.

Figure 8.23 The Invert Paper icon has been activated and the color is being applied inside the "negative space" of the texture.

2 Open the secondary image you wish to capture as a paper texture.

3 Choose Select > All, or Cmd-A (Mac)/Ctrl-A (PC).

4 Choose Edit > Copy, or Cmd-C (Mac)/Ctrl-C (PC).

5 Now make the clone copy the active image in Painter.

6 Choose Edit > Paste, or, if using the default shortcut, Cmd-Shift-V (Mac)/Ctrl-Shift-V (PC).

7 You will now see the secondary image pasted over the clone copy as an image layer listed in the Layers palette.

8 Lower the layer opacity using the Opacity slider in the Layers palette to about 50% (Figure 8.24). This allows you to see through the secondary image layer and observe how the pasted layer image relates to the underlying collage. You can move the layer around by clicking and dragging with the Layer Adjuster tool (in the top right of the Toolbox).

9 If the layer needs to be resized or rotated use the Layers > Convert to Reference Layer. Hold the Shift key down and drag in the corner control handles to rescale the reference layer. Hold the Cmd (Mac)/Ctrl (PC) key down and drag on the corner control handles to rotate the reference layer.

10 Once satisfied with the scale and position of the reference layer, return the layer opacity to 100% and save this file as a RIFF. This file could serve as a clone source template at this stage. In other words you could now return to the working image and clone from this file, knowing the source image would be of exactly the right scale and resolution.

11 With the layer selected in the Layers palette, choose Layer > Drop.

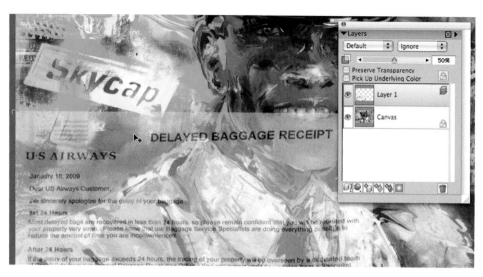

Figure 8.24 By lowering the layer opacity you can exactly position it over the collage prior to returning the layer to 100% opacity and using the resulting image as a template for a paper texture.

12 To make an effective paper texture it is best to have a high contrast black and white image. An effective way to do this is to choose Effects > Surface Control > Express Texture.

13 Experiment with the Express Texture sliders until you get a high contrast image that preserves details.

14 Choose Select > All (Cmd-A/Ctrl-A).

15 If you do not have the Papers palette showing on your Painter desktop, then choose Window > Library Palettes > Papers. You will then see the Papers palette appear.

16 Choose Capture Paper from the Papers palette pop-up menu (the small solid black triangle in top right corner of the palette). Capture Paper is the first item in the pop-up menu (not to be confused with the similarly named Make Paper which is the second item in the menu).

17 Name and save the custom paper. You will now see it appear in the Papers palette preview window.

18 With the current working image open and active, choose the Chalk > Square Chalk 35 brush variant (or choose any other grainy brush).

19 Choose Layer > New Layer. Make sure Preserve Transparency is unchecked in the Layers palette.

20 Start painting the texture into the new layer using dark colors.

21 Click on the Invert Paper icon in the Papers palette (the right-hand one of the two icons to the right of the preview window).

22 Experiment with painting into the negative space of the paper texture with light colors.

Troubleshooting and Backing Up Custom Papers

If, after naming a new custom paper and clicking OK, you get the error message: "Unable to save paper," then your current paper library is full and cannot accommodate the size of paper you are attempting to capture. Art material libraries in Painter have limited capacities and once full will not accept any new content. When you get this error message you have four choices, as described below. A combination of the following four choices will ensure you are always able to save a custom paper texture and access it again in the future.

A. Reduce the size of your paper texture source template

1 With your paper texture source template open, and before capturing your paper, choose Canvas > Resize.

2 Uncheck Constrain File Size in the Resize window.

3 Reduce the size (pixel or dimensions) of the template to 25% of the working image size before capturing the paper. This will involve a little bit of mathematics since you will have to calculate what numbers to replace the old numbers with by dividing them by 4.

4 Click OK.

5 Set the Scale slider in the Papers palette to 400% (Figure 8.25) and the paper will be of exactly the right scale to fit perfectly once in the working image (without the texture repeating or being cropped).

Figure 8.25 Adjusting the paper scale to 400% allows you to fit exactly to your image a paper template that you reduced in scale by 25%.

B. Make a new custom papers library

Whether or not you fill up your current paper library, it is important to back up your custom papers into custom paper libraries. If you don't you may lose the custom paper and you will not have convenient access to it should you wish to reuse it in the future.

1 Click on the small solid black triangle in the top right corner of the Papers palette. This accesses the Papers palette pop-up menu.

2 Select Paper Mover (Figure 8.26).

3 Click on the New button in the lower right of the Paper Mover window.

4 Name a new custom paper library and I recommend saving it into the Custom Data sub-folder in your project folder (and creating one if you don't have such a folder); that way you

Figure 8.26 Select the Paper Mover from the Papers palette pop-up menu.

keep all your custom textures with your project files. Remember when naming a custom paper library that you are not naming a single paper texture but a receptacle for a collection of different papers. I usually start with adding a "1" at the end of my custom paper library name in case I end up creating more than one for a project.

5 Click Save.

6 Now you can drag paper texture squares from the left-hand side of the Paper Mover (the catalog of current paper library), to the right-hand side (the catalog of new paper library) (Figure 8.27). This copies the textures over. If you wish to then edit the current library by deleting the duplicated custom papers you can do so.

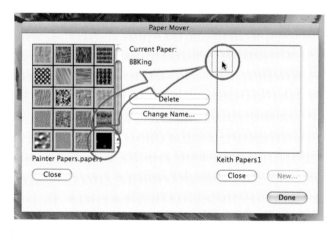

Figure 8.27 In the Paper Mover drag your custom paper from the left (current library) to the right (new paper library).

C. Change your current paper library

You can always change the current paper library. If you have a custom paper library prepared for your current project you may wish to open that. You can open any paper library, including JeremyFavePapers2.

1 Select Open Library from the Papers palette pop-up menu (solid black triangle in top right of the Papers palette). You will see a warning: "Loading a new Paper Texture will overwrite your current Painter Papers.papers (or your current Papers library name), and any changes you have made will be lost." This is warning you not to open another paper library until you have backed up any custom papers in your current library.

2 Click Load.

3 Locate the paper library you wish to open.

4 Click Open.

If you wish to return to Painter's default paper library, click on the Paper Selector menu, then click on the small solid black triangle in the top right corner of the Paper Selector pop-out menu (this is a *different* solid black triangle from the one in the top right of the Papers palette), and choose Restore Default Library which is at the very bottom of the menu (Figure 8.28). You will see a message: "Restoring to Default Library will overwrite your current library, any

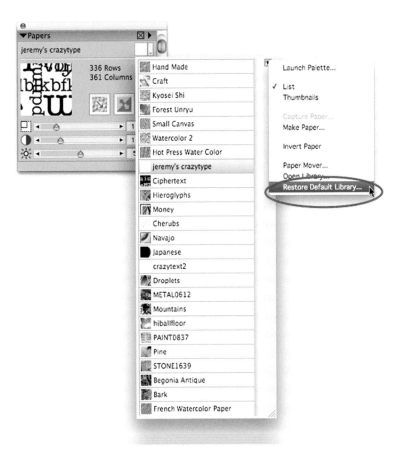

Figure 8.28 The well hidden Restore Default Library menu item! In this example the current paper library is JeremyFavePapers2.

changes will be lost." This warns you that any custom papers you haven't backed up into another paper library will be lost. Click Restore to return to the default library.

By choosing Restore Default Library the Painter papers library (the default current library when you first install Painter) would automatically become the current library.

D. Delete custom papers that you don't need anymore from your current library

1 Click on the small solid black triangle in the top right corner of the Papers palette. This accesses the Papers palette pop-up menu.

2 Select Paper Mover.

3 In the left side of the Paper Mover you see all the current paper library contents represented by small square icons.

4 Scroll down for the most recently added. Custom papers may appear as white squares.

5 Click on the squares to see their names and choose one of the custom papers you wish to delete.

6 Click on the Delete button. Be careful not to delete default papers. Only delete papers you don't need. If you think you may need a paper again in the future then it is best to back it up into a custom paper library (see below).

Stage V: Combined Media Completion—Post-Print Treatment

Before printing your collage image you will first have to decide when you are finished in Painter. Deciding this is not as easy as it may sound! Whenever you feel you have done enough to the image put it aside for a day or two and revisit it with a fresh eye. I often find that I keep developing work long after I originally thought it was finished. The more you develop your work in Painter, the more powerful and beautiful your final printed artwork will become. With collage I suggest it is better to err on the side of more digital work than less.

When you are ready to print your collage portrait, flatten your image and resave it. Add a colored border to the flat digital image and paint into this border on the digital canvas (see the section *How to Add a Painted Border for Printing* in Chapter 6). After you have printed the collage apply a fixative to the print and, if you have printed on canvas apply a transparent gel medium with physical brush stroke texture that follows the forms of the composition (see the section *Post-Print Painting* in Chapter 6). At this point in the process you have many options at your fingertips to add physical dimensionality, organic richness, more life and maximum visual impact to your artwork. You can add opaque colored acrylic or oil paint with a brush and palette knife, other types of traditional media, gold leaf, chin collé (glued paper), and so on. You can use acrylic gel medium as a glue to attach relevant, small, flat, light objects, documents and memorabilia to your print surface. To help expand your imagination and open up your world of possibilities, research the art and techniques of artists such as Romare Bearden, Joseph Cornell, Hannah Höch, Robert Rauschenberg and Kurt Schwitters.

Figure 8.29 Adding acrylic paint to the *San Francisco Heart* collage.

If you'd like to learn more about the mixed media aspects of this process you will enjoy disc three of *The Art of Collage Portraiture* DVD set which focuses on post-printing techniques, and also some of the tutorial videos on PaintboxJ.com. The PaintboxJ.com tutorials include videos of the clone source template technique, and other digital collage techniques discussed in this chapter. I run collage workshops in my studio in which you create a collage, learning both digital and traditional techniques (see JeremySutton.com for details).

In the following final chapter I share a selection of my paintings, including several examples of collage portraits that were created using the techniques described in this chapter. I include earlier stages of some of these to give you an insight into the way they transformed and the process that went into creating them. Enjoy the artwork!

I wish you much pleasure in making your own collage portraits, and experimenting and exploring with this wonderful medium of digital paint.

9

Gallery

Introduction

Enjoy this sampling of my artworks, most of which were created using the same workflow, strategies and techniques shared in this book. In some cases I have included earlier stages of my works in order to give you a better insight into my creative process. I have included relevant web page URLs from my art web site (www.jeremysutton.com) where you'll learn the story behind each work.

The artworks in this gallery are divided into three sections:

I Life Paintings;
II Paintings from Photos; and
III Collage Portraits.

These sections mirror the way my instructions develop in the book, starting with freehand observational drawing and painting exercises, moving onto painting from photographic reference, and finally concluding with the integration of multiple images into collage portraits.

Besides viewing these samples, I also invite you to view the movie called *Roll That Boogie*, featured on PaintboxJ.com, where two of my collage portrait subjects, former San Francisco Mayor Willie L. Brown and San Francisco iconoclast Robert C. Pritikin, share their reactions to their portraits. I would like to take this opportunity to thank each and every portrait subject, and everyone else involved in providing me with material and inspiration for making these artworks.

I. Portraits from Life

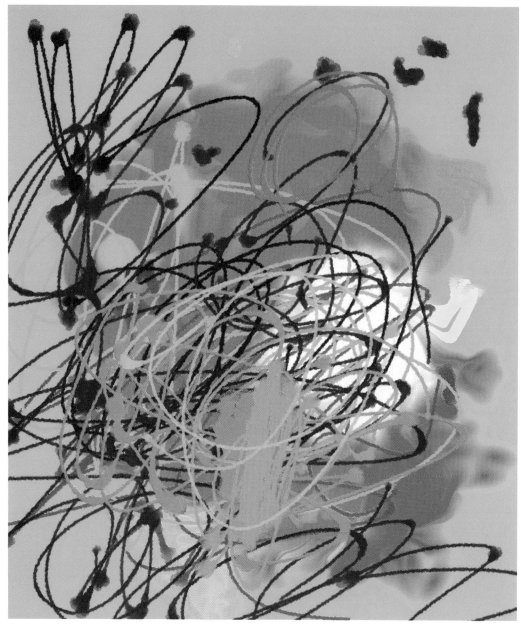

Figure 9.1 An early stage of a portrait of a young girl, Avery, painted from life at Google head-quarters in Mountain View, California, 2008. I first asked Avery to make play with Painter and then built up the portrait over her own marks.

Figure 9.2 At this intermediate stage you see the transition from energetic gestural marks towards the more precise definition of selected details, such as her eyes.

Figure 9.3 *Avery*, 20 inches by 17 inches, pigment and acrylic on canvas, 2008.

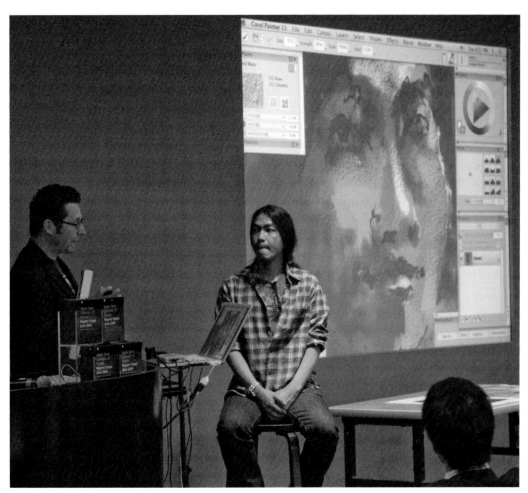

Figure 9.4 Kukaek, a "volunteer" subject from the audience, sits for his portrait as part of my presentation at the Apple Store, London, UK, 2009.

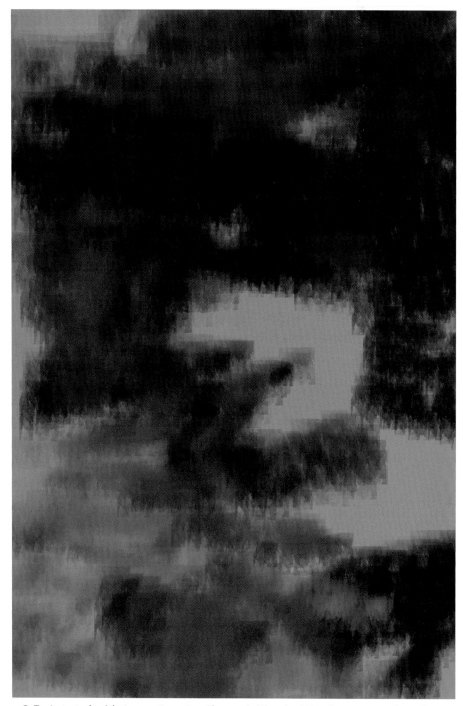

Figure 9.5 I started with JeremyFaves2 > Sherron's Blender Wood to cover a lot of canvas fast, building up the main blocks of tone.

Figure 9.6 Using the Chalks > Square Chalk 35 to refine detail.

Figure 9.7 *Kukaek*, 16 inches by 24 inches, 2009, completed with the JeremyFaves2 > Jeremy's SumiPollock Splash.

Figure 9.8 Presenting Adobe co-founder, John Warnock, with his portrait that I created from life; Tech Museum of Innovation, San Jose, California.

Figure 9.9 *Jay Stock*, 24 inches by 24 inches, pigment on fine art paper, 2003. Portrait created from a live sitting in San Francisco of legendary photographer Jay Stock (www.jeremysutton.com/jay.html). You can also listen to an interview with Jay about his life, on PaintboxJ.com

Figure 9.10 Early stage of live portrait of one of my students, Marjorie Post, who sat for a demonstration portrait during one of my Painter Creativity Seminars in San Francisco. The whole portrait was created using the Artists > Sargent Brush. This shows the early stage created with a large Sargent Brush and quick rough brush strokes.

Figure 9.11 Mid-stage as the details start to be defined through use of smaller brush size.

Figure 9.12 Marjorie Post, 2008.

Figure 9.13 Using a special "spray paint can" on an electronic wall to paint a portrait of Hugo Toland, Creative Director of Daydream Network, at the Royal Albert Hall LOAD exhibition, London, 2009.

Figure 9.14 The completed portrait of Hugo.

Figure 9.15 Drawing a traditional pencil sketch of April Madden, Deputy Editor, *Official Corel Painter Magazine*, at the Royal Albert Hall, London, 2009.

Figure 9.16 The completed sketch of April.

Figure 9.17 Creating a live digital portrait of Yorick Wilks, renowned computer scientist and Professor of Artificial Intelligence at the University of Sheffield, as part of a presentation "Chaos Versus Order: The Role of Entropy in Portraiture" at the Oxford Internet Institute, Oxford University, UK, 2009.

Figure 9.18 The portrait of Yorick was started by painting over a photo I took of him reflected in the Oxford Internet Institute sign.

Figure 9.19 Yorick Wilks, 2009.

II. Painting from Photos

Figure 9.20 *Impassioned*, 38 inches by 26 inches, pigment and acrylic on canvas, 2006 (www.jeremysutton.com/impassioned.html). This painting is based on a photograph I took of professional Argentine Tango dancers Mariana Dragone and Jaimes Friedgen when they performed at the Metronome Dance Center, San Francisco. This was a single moment in the dance that captures the intensity and passion of the connection between the two dancers, as with *Moment in Time*, also featured in this gallery.

Figure 9.21 *Jay*, 2009. This painting is based on a photograph of legendary photographer Jay Stock taken at the Imaging USA conference in Phoenix, Arizona. Note the use of empty space and unfinished edges. I wanted to convey his warm humor and depth of character.

Figure 9.22 *Groovin'*, 38 inches by 50 inches, pigment and acrylic on canvas, 2005 (www. jeremysutton.com/groovin.html). This painting is based on a photograph that I took of Manu and Kat at the "9:20 Special" weekly swing dance in San Francisco. I enjoyed playing with the brush strokes on the canvas, treating them as an extension of the dance. I like the way that Manu and Kim are looking in different directions and are yet so connected and so enjoying the playfulness of the moment.

Figure 9.23 *Carol Pucci Doll*, 38 inches by 57 inches, pigment and acrylic on canvas, 2006. This portrait was part of my *San Francisco Bay Area Women of Style* series.

Figure 9.24 *Swingout*, 52 inches by 40 inches, pigment and acrylic on canvas, 2005 (www. jeremysutton.com/swingout.html). Painting based on photograph of Damon Stone and Ruby Red dancing in San Francisco. In a "swing out," a term used in Lindy Hop and other forms of swing dancing, the follow typically swings towards and then away from their partner. What I love about the feeling in this picture is that you can sense the flow of the dance and the connection between Damon and Ruby.

Figure 9.25 *Rock*, 38 inches by 57 inches, pigment and acrylic on canvas, 2006 (www.jeremysutton.com/cityshapes-rock.html). This painting is part of a series, *Cityshapes: Motion, Body & Soul*, produced in collaboration with modern dancer Tiffany Barbarash. See also the painting *Island*, another in the series, reproduced in Chapter 7.

Figure 9.26 My painting *Waterfall* (featured extensively as a case study in Chapters 4 and 5) started with some simple calligraphic black brush strokes on a plain white canvas.

Figure 9.27 An intermediate stage of *Waterfall*. The calligraphic brush strokes were eventually covered up as I added more and more color, texture and detail.

Figure 9.28a *Waterfall*, 24 inches by 36 inches, pigment and acrylic on canvas, 2009 (www.jeremysutton.com/waterfall.html). This painting was inspired by a photograph I took in GuangZhou, China. The chop (red stamp) on the upper left is my name in ancient Chinese characters. The poem on the lower right is inscribed in the rock next to the waterfall and means, roughly, a good friend is never distant.

Figure 9.28b *Waterfall* (detail). Note the loose, almost abstract, way the Koi fish have been depicted and the use of brush strokes to convey movement. Also note the variety of colors used throughout to add a sense of depth to the water and reflectivity to the water surface.

Figure 9.28c *Waterfall* (detail). See how the vertical dripping brushwork in the waterfall gives a sense of downward movement, which contrasts with the solid dabbed rock and foliage brushwork surrounding it.

III. Collage Portraits

Figure 9.29 The beginning stage of the company portrait *Reynolds & Brown.* The assignment was to create a symbolic portrayal of the company Reynolds & Brown, including depictions of the founders, the company headquarters, mascot, logo, flag and scenes from when the company was launched. Notice how I built up the composition with an underlying photo-montage.

Figure 9.30 Here you see the ivy wall and various woodcut layers added as overlays to the developing collage. Notice how layers have been reduced in prominence to varying degrees by lowering the layer opacity. This in turn allows certain visual elements to become the main focal points while other elements fade into the background.

Figure 9.31 *Reynolds & Brown,* 40 inches by 60 inches, pigment and acrylic on canvas, 2009 (www.jeremysutton.com/reynoldsandbrown.html). More Artists > Impressionist brush strokes were added, gradually transforming the photomontage into a painting.

Figure 9.32 *Free at Last,* 45 inches by 30 inches, pigment and acrylic on canvas, 2003. This portrait is a tribute to the way that Nelson Mandela led his country into a peaceful transition to democracy. The collage includes the original first 1994 ballot form that features Mandela's smiling face, and portraits of him from when he was a lawyer in the 1950s, through to his release from prison on February 11, 1990. Mandela's handprint is included, which has the map of Africa in it.

Figure 9.33 The early stage of the portrait of former San Francisco Mayor, Joseph L. Alioto. Note in this case, unlike the *Reynolds & Brown* portrait, I started with a painting and then added photographic elements later.

Figure 9.34 A later stage of the Alioto portrait in which I am introducing more elements into the background, using a painterly approach.

Figure 9.35 *Mayor Joseph L. Alioto*, 96 inches by 114 inches, pigment and acrylic on canvas, 2009 (www.jeremysutton.com/mayoralioto.html). This portrait of former San Francisco Mayor, Joseph L. Alioto, was originally created as part of the San Francisco Legendary Mayors series. Included in the painting are many visual elements, some political and some personal, including excerpts from a letter Alioto wrote to his daughter Angela on her graduation as a lawyer, the invite to his inauguration, a mayoral campaign button from 1967, the nationally recognized Transamerica Building (the creation of which Mayor Alioto vigorously supported during his tenure), and the Certificate of Commemoration printed for Alioto's historic early morning 1906 San Francisco Earthquake Observance at City Hall, April 18, 1969, and many other images.

Figure 9.36a *Portrait of Robert C. Pritikin*, 38 inches by 57 inches, pigment, acrylic and miscellaneous items on canvas, 2005 (www.jeremysutton.com/bob.html). This portrait was the case study used in my DVD set *The Art of Collage Portraiture*. The portrait features Bob's family and highlights from his life in advertising, his book and many friends.

Figure 9.36b Bob Pritikin admiring his portrait, San Francisco, 2005.

Figure 9.37 My portrait of Giles Henderson, Master of Pembroke College, Oxford, 2006.

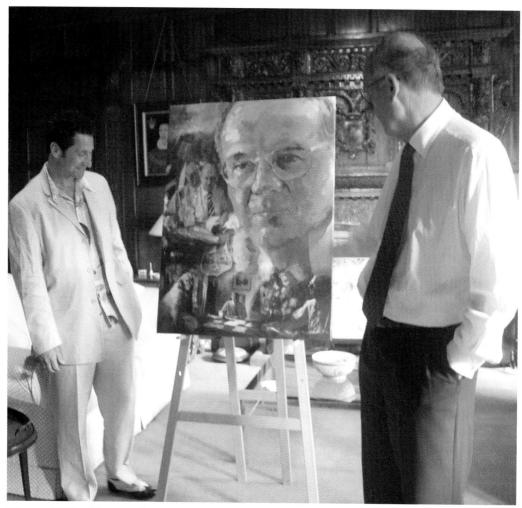

Figure 9.38 *Giles Henderson, Master of Pembroke College, Oxford University,* 30 inches by 40 inches, pigment and acrylic on canvas, 2006 (www.jeremysutton.com/gileshenderson.html). This portrait of Mr Giles I. Henderson CBE, BCL, MA, the current Master of my Alma Mater, was presented to the Pembroke College Art Collection on June 23, 2006. I studied Physics at Pembroke College from 1979 to 1982. The painting captures many aspects of Giles' life, both personal and professional, including views of him working at his desk in his capacity as Master of Pembroke College, his beautiful dog Ellie, the college crest, the Pembroke Chapel Quad, and his family on the occasion of his being presented with the Commander of the British Empire (CBE) by Queen Elizabeth II.

Figure 9.39 Early "muck up" stage of portrait of Dame Stephanie Shirley.

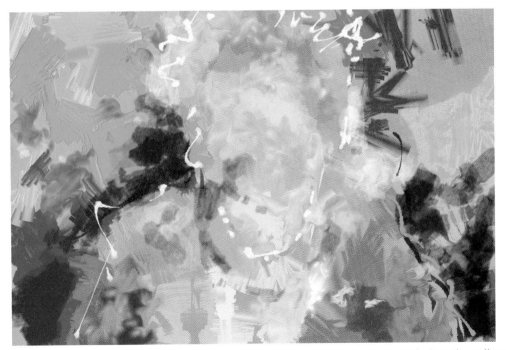

Figure 9.40 Further development of the painted background prior to introducing the collage elements.

Figure 9.41 *Dame Stephanie Shirley*, 36 inches by 24 inches, pigment and acrylic on canvas, 2009 (www.jeremysutton.com/dameshirley.html). This portrait of pioneering entrepreneur and philanthropist Dame Stephanie Shirley was created as part of a lecture I gave in 2008 at the Oxford Internet Institute, an institute that Dame Stephanie endowed in 2001. I was demonstrating the differences and parallels between creating a digital portrait from life (direct observation) versus from a photographic reference.

Figure 9.42 *The Speech—Portrait of Barack Obama,* 40 inches by 57 inches, pigment and acrylic on canvas, 2008 (www.jeremysutton.com/obama.html). This portrait was inspired by Barack Obama's speech accepting the Democratic nomination for President, at the Democratic Convention, delivered on August 28th, 2008, at Invesco Field stadium in front of an estimated 84,000 people. Watching on television, I used my iPhone to capture images from the speech. I used these images as the reference photos used to create this collage portrait.

Figure 9.43 *Rick and His Buick Beauty*, 24 inches by 20 inches, pigment and acrylic on canvas, 2007 (www.jeremysutton.com/buick.html). This portrait of Rick and newly detailed and renovated 1938 Buick convertible was taken outside his Art Deco Oakland home on the shores of Lake Merritt. The painting features the Buick 8 logo he designed and the special red and yellow hub cub trimming he added. Also featured are depictions of him and his lovely wife Laurie, and him playing with his band The Martini Brothers at the historic Lake Merritt Hotel.

Figure 9.44 *Song for Peace—Portrait of Yitzhak Rabin*, 30 inches by 40 inches, pigment and acrylic on canvas, 1996 (www.jeremysutton.com/rabin.html). This portrait of the former Israeli Prime Minister Yitzhak Rabin is a combination of a freehand painting and a collage of symbolic images. After Rabin was assassinated I saw the stark image of a bloodied song sheet with a bullet hole through it on the front page of the British newspaper, *The European*. The song was Shir Ha-Shalom (Song for Peace), a peace song from the sixties that Rabin had just joined in singing with the crowd at the peace rally in Tel Aviv immediately before he was killed.

Figure 9.45 *Mississippi Goddam—Portrait of Nina Simone,* 40 inches by 60 inches, pigment and acrylic on canvas, 2006 (www.jeremysutton.com/mississippigoddamn.html). I was inspired to create this portrait after hearing Kim Nalley's beautiful and moving rendition of Nina Simone's seminal protest song of pain and hope, *Mississippi Goddamn,* during her performance of the Nina Simone songbook at the Fillmore Fair, San Francisco, in 2005. The painting includes visual references, made in the song, to the murder of four young girls in the bombing of the Sixteenth Street Baptist Church in Birmingham, Alabama, on September 15th, 1963, and the murder of civil rights worker Medgar Evers in Mississippi on June 12, 1963.

Figure 9.46 *Tribute to Frankie Manning*, 38 inches by 54 inches, pigment and acrylic on canvas, 2009 (www.jeremysutton.com/frankie.html). This portrait is a tribute to the legendary Lindy Hopper, pioneering dancer and ambassador of Lindy Hop swing dancing around the world, Frankie Manning, who sadly left us just short of his 95th birthday, which was celebrated in New York City (the Frankie 95 Birthday Festival). Frankie was a wonderful man, an inspiration to me and many thousands of other Lindy Hop dancers across the world.

Figure 9.47 *Dad*, 2005, 24 inches by 30 inches, in memory of my father, Maurice Sutton (www.jeremysutton.com/dad.html). This is a portrait of my father, Maurice Sutton, who died in December 1988. I dedicate this portrait in loving memory to my Dad.

Conclusion

I wish you much joy, pleasure and satisfaction in pursuing your creative endeavors, and, if you are a creative professional, much success too. I hope you have enjoyed this book and that my suggestions have been helpful to you.

Happy painting!

Cheers,

Jeremy

Appendix : Student Gallery

This book grew out of a class workbook I developed in the 1990s. It wouldn't exist without the thousands of wonderful students I have taught over the years, whose input, questions, enthusiasm, artwork and inspiration have been my guide and motivation to writing the *Painter Creativity: Digital Artist's Handbook* series. I wish to take this opportunity to thank my former and current students, all of whom I am so proud! As much as I would have liked to feature artwork from all my students, with space being limited, I have instead invited four of my Master Students to share a small sampling of their work, some created during my workshops and some created in their own studios. All four have studied with me multiple times over many years, and are members of my Master Forum group. Their styles and subject matter differ from the examples shared in this book and can thus provide you with a broader spectrum of ideas.

The artworks in this gallery are based on photographic reference and my students have kindly included their original source images and intermediate "muck up" stages to help give you a sense of the process involved in getting to the final digital paintings. Please note that, as with all other imagery in this book, the photographs and paintings in this gallery are copyrighted by the artists and may not be used as a basis for creating derivative works. The commentary from the artists gives you more insight into how they were created. Notice which brushes they have used (you may recognize some) and how they build up the paintings and use color.

In many cases the artists featured here took their work to another level, not shown here, with the addition of physical media to their prints. Lois, for instance, added her father's surveying instruments to the collage she made of him.

Enjoy the gallery. I hope you find their work as inspirational as I do.

Works by Henk Dawson

Figure A2.1 *Beach*, original source photograph.

Figure A2.2 *Beach*, "muck up" stage.

Figure A2.3 *Beach*, final digital painting. "All three paintings of mine featured in this gallery are from the *Painting Curacao* project I did in April 2009 while vacationing on this beautiful small Caribbean island. With months of gray skies in the Northwest (when I painted foggy dreamy scenes and longed for sunshine), I went to Curacao and was awakened and inspired by the bright colors and the sunlight of the island. In this case I took a picture of people enjoying the beautiful beach. The photo did not capture the mood of people having a good time. The loud music is not in the picture. I envisioned a painting which brings out the elements of joy, fun, and music. I needed vibrant impressionistic colors and impressionistic brushwork. I mucked up the photo with the Artists > Impressionist brush using not too large a brush size, mainly continuing with this brush throughout the painting. At some point I added the Underpainting > Impressionist Color Scheme and edited it to fade the effect. Still using the same brush I painted with color variability in RGB. In the end I added Sherron's Blender Wood from the JeremyGuestFaves4 brush category to shake up the water a bit with low stylus pressure (great with the Intuos 4)."

Figure A2.4 *Boat,* original source photograph.

Figure A2.5 *Boat,* "muck up" stage.

Figure A2.6 *Boat,* final digital painting. "I took a picture of a small boat which I found quite beautiful, but sterile, and decided to make it quite hazy, mucking it up with the Acrylics Capture Bristle. I then used the Artists > Impressionist brush to build up detail, and finally added color variability in RGB using the same brush."

Figure A2.7 *Market,* original source photograph.

Figure A2.8 *Market,* "muck up" stage.

Figure A2.9 *Market,* final digital painting. "I took a photograph of the market and did not increase the contrast or saturation as the photo was already quite colorful and I liked the subtle color nuances. Using Painter 11 I started the muck up phase with Auto-Painting, Smart Stroke Painting and Smart Settings with the Artists Impressionist Brush, stopping it early on, and continuing with my own large brush strokes and colors using the same brush. Selective detail was brought in with the Artists > Sargent Brush and blended with JeremyGuestFaves4 > Sherron's Blender Wood. I found the enhanced sensitivity of the Intuos 4 fantastic to build up brush stroke upon brush stroke using very light pressure, like slowly accumulating multiple thin layers of paint. Some finishing touches were done with the Impressionist Brush, again with low pressure."

Works by Lois Freeman-Fox

Figure A2.10 *LoraRose,* original source photograph.

Figure A2.11 *LoraRose,* "muck up" stage.

Figure A2.12 *LoraRose,* final digital painting. "The painting was inspired by a photograph in a newspaper of an older woman sitting in a chair with a younger woman looking through a window at her. I always thought the image applied really well to my family ancestor series. The original consists of three images: the newspaper photo, a photo of my grandmother gardening, and a photo of her granddaughter, Lora. At first I was going to take my Grandmother Rose and put her in the chair, with her daughter, Freddie, looking on but I decided instead to use an old and faded photograph of my cousin Lora (Rose's granddaughter) coming down a staircase in my apartment in NY that I took 30 years ago. The picture of my grandmother Rose is black and white so the first challenge was to work with color. With your help, I tried many different kinds of fill with varying degrees of transparency. This helped me solve one of my main problems in working with old photographs, which is their intrinsic black and white quality. I used a fairly wide combination of Big Wet Luscious, Sargent, Retrodots, Soft Cloner, Just Add Water and Sumi-e, working back and forth between the abstraction of the color and the realism of the photograph."

Figure A2.13 *God Is Time*, original source photograph.

Figure A2.14 *God Is Time*, "muck up" stage.

Figure A2.15a *God Is Time,* final digital painting. "This collage was created in Jeremy's fabulous Collage Master Class. It is a portrait of my father, Clarence Freeman. The main image is based on a photo I took of him six months before he died at the age of 90. It was inspired by a poem he wrote about evolution:

> Quoth God, "It is clear I am time.
> With evolution the power is mine.
> I'm no Omnipotent Watchmaker,
> Nor Benevolent Caretaker.
> Life sprang from primordial slime."
> —Clarence Freeman

In preparation for this master class I scanned documents, photographs, drawings, objects, poems, I uncovered postcards my father sent to me as a child and a "bull—t" stamp he saved in addition to the stamp he used to certify his engineering drawings. It was a labor of love. After it was done and printed in the workshop I painted it with acrylic paint, pinned his favorite tie tac (a fish with legs that says "Darwin" on it), and attached a slide rule, a couple of watches, a level, a Senior Olympic swimming medal, fossils, gold dust, shells and some other engineering tools he used. I built a simple, sturdy wooden frame around it.

Figure A2.15b *God Is Time*, the final physical collage artwork, including objects attached, hanging in a Red, White, and Blue show at the Government Center in Ventura, California, 2009. The brushes and techniques used in this artwork included everything we learned in the collage class, such as making nozzles out of objects, expressing texture, capturing paper textures, using photos as paper textures, using inverted paper textures, cloning and composite methods as well as using Painter's arsenal of brushes. The post-production workshop in acrylics given by Peggy Gyulai was also informative and inspiring and helped in the making of this collage."

Works by Sam Gray

Figure A2.16 *Gatsby*, original source photograph.

Figure A2.17 *Gatsby*, "muck up" stage.

Figure A2.18 *Gatsby*, final digital painting. "In the Fall of 2007 I was with Jeremy at the Great Gatsby Impressionist Master Workshop. We spent the day at Dunsmuir Estate in Oakland, California. What a breathtaking experience. We were picked up at the gate in a vintage car playing 1920s music. I felt like I had stepped back in time or was on a movie set. There were images to take by the hundreds; I took a thousand that day. This was one that set the tone for the day. I used a mixture of brushes to give me the mood that I wanted. I like blending brushes to create textures and depth."

Figure A2.19 *Monterosso Bike*, montage showing the original source photograph and several stages of the painting.

Figure A2.20 *Monterosso Bike,* final digital painting. "This art piece was taken in Cinque Terra, Italy, in a small town on the coast. I noticed this abandoned bike just sitting there with flat tires just waiting for me. To most people the life had gone out of this bike, but I saw that it still had potential to bring joy. I captured the image knowing that one day I could come back and enjoy the ride again. The final painting is a 30 × 45 Master Oil Interpretive Painting on canvas."

Figure A2.21 *Red Umbrella,* original source photograph.

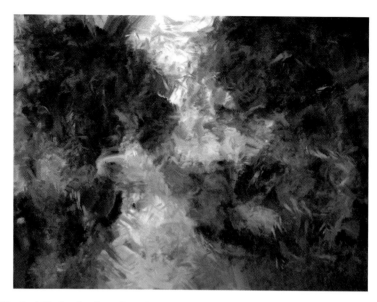

Figure A2.22 *Red Umbrella,* "muck up" stage.

Figure A2.23 *Red Umbrella,* final digital painting. "I enjoy capturing art anytime, rain or shine. Some of the best images are in unusual and bad weather. I was out with a friend in San Francisco and was struck with the lines in this scene. I didn't like the construction scaffolding in the background, or that I didn't have a subject in the foreground, but the lines were a good start. I capture scenes and bank them knowing that I can complete them at a later date. Digital photography has made my work come alive and gives me the opportunity to perfect an image or painting that was not possible earlier in my career. On another rainy day I happened to see a lady walking down the street with a red umbrella, and I followed her for a short time waiting for just the right light. When she walked under the marquis of a hotel entrance the overhead bright light hit her umbrella and it came alive. That was the shot I had been looking for to complete this painting. I simply painted out the scaffolding then used brushes with an Impressionistic style and my image was complete. In 2007 I entered the PPA (Professional Photographers of America) competition for the first time in 11 years. The judges seemed to like what I was doing and all four of my images went into the Loan Collection."

Works by Jolyn Montgomery

Figure A2.24 *Divan Japonais*, original source photograph.

Figure A2.25 *Divan Japonais*, "muck up" stage.

Figure A2.26 *Divan Japonais,* final digital painting. "This was created during Jeremy's Great Gatsby Impressionist Workshop. I was inspired by the style of Henri Toulouse-Lautrec and wanted to create a scene that had the same feel as Toulouse-Lautrec's work. I used the same background from the *Elsa* painting (below) for this one. The source of the texture was ballgowns on a clothing rack. Keeping backgrounds you like in a separate file is a great resource to turn to. I created a full size paper texture template to add the calligraphic script on the left of the painting. I also used a Spotlight effect to give the painting the feeling that the ladies were lit up from the stage lights."

Figure A2.27 *Elsa,* original source photograph.

Figure A2.28 *Elsa,* "muck up" stage.

Figure A2.29 *Elsa,* final digital painting. "The full title of this painting is *The Life and Times of Elsa and her Friends*. I made this painting during one of Jeremy's collage workshops. During the creative process I ended up making 39 layers, including paper textures, multiple images and glazing. Collage is a wonderful technique to have. Sometimes I find that images supplied by a client are too old, too small, or too out of focus to be used in a fine art piece as a single painting. With collage you can bring all of the client's loved images together and create a treasured painting."

Figure A2.30 *Roper,* original source photograph.

Figure A2.31 *Roper,* "muck up" stage.

Figure A2.32 *Roper,* final digital painting. "This is a portrait of Roper, a retired cow roping horse. He was painted in one of Jeremy's Working with Color workshops. My client wanted a slightly abstract painting with lot of color but with a clear definition of Roper's dorsal strip, which is a main characteristic of the buckskin horse."

Index